5S
for Safety

IMPLEMENTATION TOOLKIT
PARTICIPANT GUIDE

CRC Press
Taylor & Francis Group
Boca Raton London New York

CRC Press is an imprint of the
Taylor & Francis Group, an **informa** business

A PRODUCTIVITY PRESS BOOK

CRC Press
Taylor & Francis Group
6000 Broken Sound Parkway NW, Suite 300
Boca Raton, FL 33487-2742

© 2000 by Taylor & Francis Group, LLC
CRC Press and Productivity Press are imprints of
Taylor & Francis Group, an informa business

No claim to original U.S. Government works
Printed in the United States of America on acid-free paper
16 15 14 13 12 11 10 9 8

International Standard Book Number-13: 978-1-4200-7592-2 (Softcover)
Created by the Productivity Press Development Team
Cover design by Rochelle Browne

Library of Congress Cataloging-in-Publication Data

5S for Safety implementation toolkit : a facilitator Guide / Productivity Development Team.
    p.   cm.
Includes bibliographical references and index
ISBN 1-4200-7592-6
1. Industrial Safety.   I. Productivity Development Team (Productivity Press)
T55.A115   2000
658.3'82—dc21   00-034158

**Visit the Taylor & Francis Web site at
http://www.taylorandfrancis.com**

**and the CRC Press Web site at
http://www.crcpress.com**

This Participant Guide is intended to help you implement the 5S for Safety System. It provides a step by step method for implementation, including checklists, worksheets, and forms. It is designed for systematic and complete implementation on the shop floor.

The 5S System has gained world wide recognition as a set of universal principles that help companies achieve and sustain high performance. For nearly two decades Productivity has helped companies implement the 5S System in their plants.

An important question always seems to surface. *How can 5S be used to improve safety?* At Productivity we have learned that it's not enough to add a sixth S, safety, and proceed as usual. Even though a basic 5S program helps improve safety, it does not prevent the causes of accidents. To do so a *Focused 5S* program is necessary.

Basic 5S is a *"fix-it"* approach. Basic 5S targets an area, sorts out unnecessary items, sets them in order, shines and inspects through cleaning, standardizes these conditions, and sustains the gains through self-discipline. In can solve up to 50% of your safety problems.

Focused 5S for Safety is a *control and prevent* approach. It performs an extensive shopfloor safety audit, and targets the causes of safety accidents, incidents, and near misses. It then helps participants eliminate unsafe conditions and behaviors before they occur by using best practices and visual controls. The *5S for Safety Implementation Toolkit* provides proven implementation strategies and techniques for maximizing both Basic 5S and Focused 5S initiatives.

Your team's 5S for Safety activities will be most effective if assisted by a facilitator using the accompanying Facilitator Guide. If your team is not assisted by a facilitator, refer to the Facilitator Guide. It provides detailed information about the entire system as well as a glossary, a section on how to use various tools and techniques, and master forms. The Facilitator Guide CD-ROM includes a PowerPoint training presentation about the 5S for Safety system and electronic versions of all forms in this toolkit. It is an integral part of this package.

Acknowledgments

The 5S for Safety Participant Guide was developed and written by Thomas Fabrizio of Productivity Press with a great deal of assistance from Janice Kuntz of Primus, Inc. The design and prepress process was managed by Lorraine Millard, also of Productivity Press.

Contents

Purpose of the Participant Guide

The purpose of the Participant Guide is to provide team members with a quick reference to 5S for Safety activities. The Participant Guide provides an overview of the process of implementing 5S for Safety including both Basic and Focused 5S.

How to Use This Participant Guide

One copy of the Participant Guide should be given to each participant at, or prior to, the beginning of the first meeting.

The Participant Guide is divided into seven modules in addition to this Introduction. Each module corresponds to one of the seven implementation steps and is designed with the same components:

• Introduction to the module

• Objectives for the step

• Information about the step with useful tips about implementation

• Application tasks

• Worksheets

To get the most out of this guide use it in the following way:

• As part of Step 1 you should attend a seminar or study group so that you understand the 5S for Safety process and tools. The module for Step 1 can help in this regard.

• Before each meeting you should read the module for the step you will be using.

• The list of application tasks will give clear directions about the tasks necessary to complete the step.

• The worksheets provide you with your own copy of the detailed activities. Keep these for yourself and use copies from the Facilitator Guide for actual implementation. Additional copies of all the toolkit forms can be printed from the files on the Facilitator Guide CD-ROM. (Filenames are in the bottom left corner of the forms.)

• For best results, you should use the Participant Guide information in the sequence provided.

Overview of Contents

Building a successful team takes effort and leadership. There are necessary tasks that the Safety Manager, Team Leader, team members and Facilitator are responsible for throughout the project.

The 5S for Safety Toolkit uses a Roadmap (see Figure 1) together with a Responsibility Matrix (see Figure 2). The Roadmap provides an at-a-glance overview of the process. The Responsibility Matrix provides more information about the individual steps, team members, and members' responsibilities.

A 7-Step Implementation Strategy

The 5S for Safety uses 7 steps to fulfill its objectives.

Step 1: Learn About 5S for Safety. The purpose of this step is to provide the required awareness and information for managers, team leaders, and participants to "buy in" and launch 5S for Safety.

Step 2: Plan and Prepare. The purpose of this step is to transfer responsibility for target projects to project teams by identifying target areas, choosing project leaders, and creating team charters.

Step 3: Form a Team. In this step project teams are formed and take over implementation of the 5S for Safety process.

Step 4: Perform Basic 5S. By performing a workplace scan and implementing Basic 5S (Sort, Set in Order, Shine, Standardize, and Sustain) the workplace is organized and up to 50% of the safety problems are removed.

Step 5: See and Think for Safety. By performing an in-depth safety audit and analyzing the data you will develop a true picture of safety conditions in your area.

Step 6: Implement Best Practices. In this step you will brainstorm, select, test, and adopt practices that will control safety conditions.

Step 7: Achieve Adherence. In this step you will create standards for best practices and ensure that they will be adhered to.

5S for Safety Roadmap

Figure 1. 5S for Safety Roadmap

Responsibility Matrix

Responsibility Matrix						
Step	Action	General Management	Safety Manager	Safety Management Team	Project Team Leader	Project Team
1	Prioritize Safety and Establish Support	X	X	X		
1	Adopt 5S for Safety Program	X	X	X	X	
2	Choose Target Area and Project Leader	X	X	X	X	
2	Conduct Preliminary Audit		X	X	X	
3	Form a Team		X	X	X	X
3	Launch Project	X	X	X	X	X
3	Create Action Plan				X	X
4	Implement Basic 5S: Rapid or In-Depth				X	X
5	Create 5S for Safety Plan				X	X
5	Conduct In-Depth Safety Audit of Target Area				X	X
5	Analyze Data				X	X
6	Brainstorm and Select Best Practice Solution				X	X
6	Implement, Test, and Adopt Solution				X	X
7	Achieve Adherence to Best Practices	X	X	X	X	X
	Celebrate Success and Completion of Project	X	X	X	X	X
	Continue Improvement Process: Restart at Step 2	X	X	X	X	X

Figure 2. 5S for Safety Responsibility Matrix

Keys to Successful Implementation

There are five keys to successfully implementing 5S for Safety.

Key One: Control Workplace Conditions

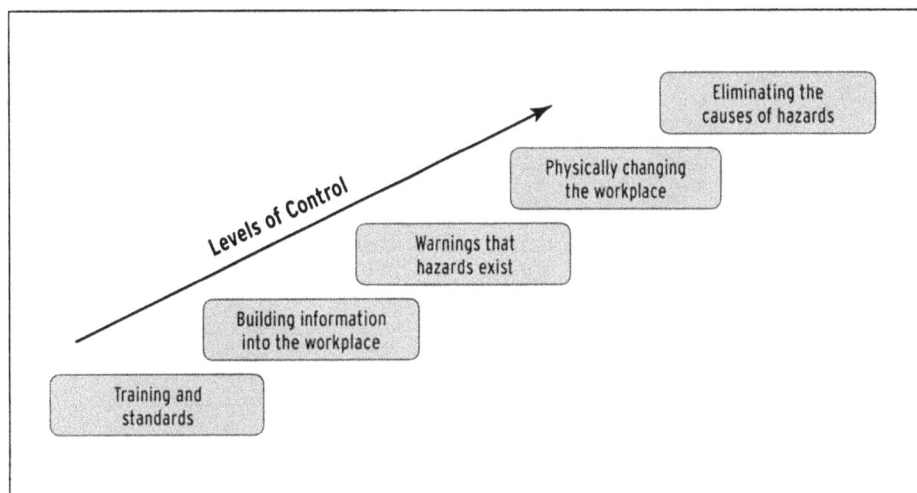

Figure 3. Levels of Control

Don't let the workplace control you—control the workplace. About 95% of workplace accidents are due to common causes. A **common cause*** is one that an individual cannot eliminate alone through safe behavior. The cause of the accident is found in workplace conditions and processes.

Be proactive, not reactive. Proactive behaviors result in measurable improvements to the safety of your workplace. Anticipating and correcting the conditions that result in problems before they occur is proactive. Start now—you can't afford to wait.

---

*Terms appearing in **bold** type are defined in the Facilitator Guide's glossary.

Key Two: Organize and Standardize Your Workplace Using the Basic 5S System

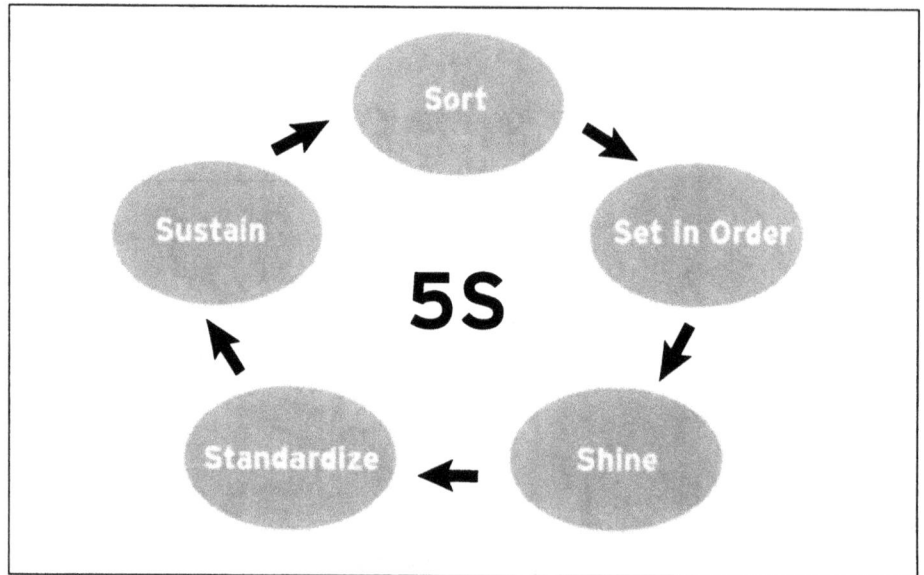

Figure 4. Basic 5S

Use Basic 5S, or an alternative housekeeping program, to keep your workplace organized, orderly, and clean.

Make Basic 5S an easily understood and automatic part of your day-to-day schedule

Key Three: Follow a Scientific and Systematic Approach to Improvement

Use a systematic method to define, document, and analyze all information. If you do not follow a systematic process, important data or information may be overlooked. Small omissions often have huge consequences.

Demonstrate leadership and technical expertise by following a consistent and proven method: Prepare, Scan, Analyze, Identify, and Implement.

Ask questions and document your findings.

> **A Scientific Approach**
>
> *See* the problems
>
> *Think* about causes
>
> *Plan* and learn from others
>
> *Do it!* But with a plan

See the problems: Use the safety audit process and tools to identify both obvious and hidden safety problems. These problems are imbedded in shopfloor conditions.

Think about the causes: Causes of safety problems are often found in our blind spots. These are the areas that we commonly overlook. 5S for Safety gives us a way to dig down and uncover the causes of problems we do not see.

Plan and learn from others: The advancement of technology provides resources for researching best practices, benchmarking other organizations' achievements, and uncovering trends and industry changes that may impact your organization.

Just do it! But with a plan: Now when you implement solutions they are based on sound thinking and represent reliable methods that have proven to be effective.

Key Four: Foster and Reward Teamwork

Figure 5. The Full Power of Teams

Use **Total Employee Involvement** (TEI) to tap into all levels of knowledge and experience in your organization. TEI brings area-specific knowledge together and integrates this cross section of knowledge, best practices, and management support into the workplace.

Key Five: Continue to Improve

Did you notice that the 5S for Safety Roadmap in Figure 1 did not have a "Stop" point? Continuous improvement is more than implementing a tool or technique one time. It includes adopting the tools as an everyday function of your job. Everyone should be a safety champion.

Summary

5S for Safety applies the 5S system in two phases. It begins with Basic 5S to organize and standardize the workplace. Then it applies Focused 5S for Safety.

The *5S for Safety Implementation Toolkit* is designed for organizations that actively set improvement goals and work toward those goals. These are the organizations whose management teams clearly understand the reasons why systems for continuous safety improvements are necessary. These are the organizations that actively commit to safety improvements.

The Toolkit delivers strategies, processes, and tools for creating and implementing reliable, proven, and effective safety improvements.

Introduction

Step 1 is divided into two primary activities: learning and sharing.

Participants start learning about 5S for Safety though seminars and study groups led by the Facilitator or other experts in the field.

Once a solid foundation is established, the group embarks upon sharing this information with coworkers and key stakeholders. This activity initiates more discussion within the organization and eventually leads to asking the organization to support further implementation.

Objectives for Step 1

The Safety Manager, 5S for Safety Champion, and Project Team Leaders and Members will:

- Understand the definition and purpose of each S in 5S.
- Understand the purpose for each of the 7 steps in the implementation process.
- Understand the keys to a successful implementation of a 5S for Safety program.
- Personally commit to implementing the process.
- Be prepared to launch Step 2 of the process.

Application Tasks

- Thoroughly study information in this step prior to your first meeting.
- Attend study groups or seminars to learn about 5S for Safety.
- Commit to your role in the implementation of the 5S for Safety.

About the 5S for Safety Method

A Focus on Safety

Poor safety conditions exist in all businesses. Accidents, incidents, and near misses are the direct results of these conditions. The 5S for Safety program focuses on identifying and eliminating hazardous conditions before an accident occurs.

Dramatic injuries hold our attention. However, did you know that for every serious accident there are approximately 29 minor accidents and 300 near misses? The workplace may not be safe, even when an accident hasn't occurred.

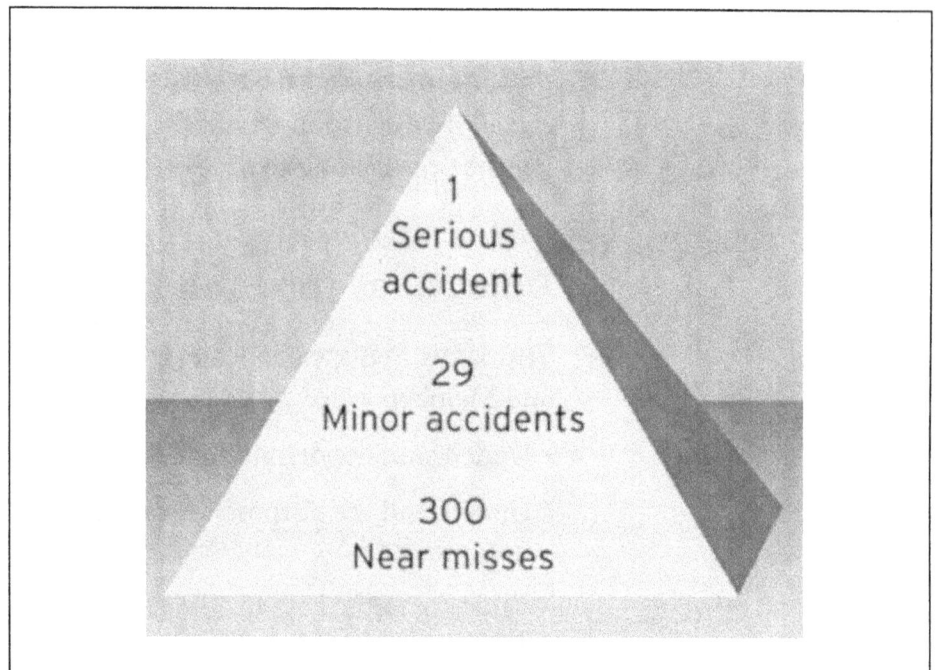

Figure 6. Accident Pyramid

There are hazardous situations that exist everywhere. Some are obvious and are easily fixed—like cleaning up a spill as soon as it happens.

Other hazards are the result of behaviors that we commonly accept, such as moving machine parts. Even detergents and chemical cleaners can be toxic. The challenge here lies in identifying the condition and then changing it so that it won't recur. It is then that changing behavior can have a lasting effect.

Implementing improvements that require a change to the organization's culture takes more time and effort. However, these changes often have the most substantial and longest lasting impact on eliminating accidents, incidents, and near misses.

Safety Improvement Principles

5S for Safety is a reliable method built on prevention and total employee involvement. It prevents accidents by controlling unnoticed near misses and neglected conditions in the work place. An accident is a problem that has already happened, and a near miss is just an accident where no one was hurt.

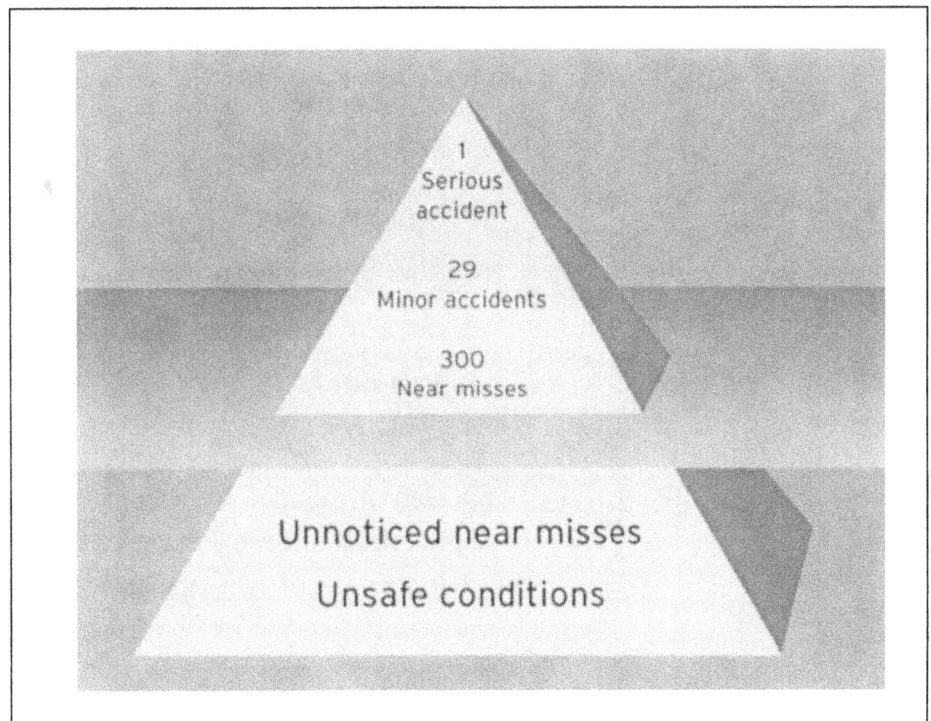

Figure 7. Accident Pyramid

The principles of Safety Improvement are:

1. Be proactive, not reactive. Of course you should discover and correct the causes of problems when they happen, but just as important is to solve those problems before they occur. You can't afford to wait.

2. The causes of safety problems exist on the shop floor—they are always there. However, they are our blind spots. Blind spots need to be identified every day.

3. Remove the causes of all accidents and near misses. Remove them or the problem will return.

4. Always involve workers in safety. Workers are closest to the facts, and have the most to lose.

5. Use a systematic method for improvement. If you're not systematic you will be overwhelmed by the task in front of you.

6. Start now. Everyone should begin to make small improvements and continue to do so every day. If this can't happen, question your strategy—it is probably flawed.

Safety Improvement Principles

1. Be proactive

2. Identify blind spots

3. Remove causes

4. Always involve workers

5. Use a systematic method

6. Start now!

People are not robots. They can't sustain a high level of concentration for long periods of time. People will always be accident prone. But we can no longer afford even one accident. When we understand this one fact our entire perspective changes. We realize that people are safe only when the environment is safe.

**The 5S for
Safety System**

Many companies, in many industries, are turning to improvement approaches such as *Lean Production, Total Productive Maintenance (TPM),* or *Total Quality Management (TQM)* to maintain and improve the high performance output. No matter what kind of industry you work in, there are five universal activities for achieving high performance. These activities are known as the 5S's.

Workplace Organization and Standardization

The purpose of the 5S System is to organize and standardize the workplace. It is accomplished in two phases: Basic 5S and Focused 5S. In both phases it is crucial that everyone understands the meaning of the 5S's.

Sort

Sort means organize—sorting needed items from unneeded items and removing the unneeded. Many workplaces are filled with a clutter of tools, parts, papers, boxes, broken items—a hodgepodge of useful things and things kept without a good reason. This mess makes it difficult to find the things needed for work and causes accidents.

Organization begins by deciding what you don't need. A method called *Red Tagging* is used to implement Sort. In Red Tagging people inspect their own workplace and place a red sticker on every item that doesn't really need to be there. Then the items are removed to another place, sold, or thrown out.

Set in Order

Set in Order means orderliness. In 5S, Set in Order means finding the best ways to store things so you always know where they are and can retrieve them easily.

Orderliness requires a system of location indicators such as clear labeling, signboards, shelf labels, etc. Specific, labeled storage places are created, and objects are labeled with "return addresses" so they are returned to the right place. Outlines of objects, painted floor marks for cart or pallet storage, and many other visual approaches help keep things where they belong.

Shine

Shine means to clean. Sweep floors, wipe off equipment, and make sure everything in the workplace stays clean. Cleanliness impacts the organization's ability to deliver high quality products to customers on time. It also detects and removes many recurring safety problems.

Standardize

Standardize differs from sort, set in order, and shine—all of which are activities. In contrast, Standardize represents the state that exists when the other three activities are continually maintained.

Standardize means finding ways to make the conditions of Sort, Set in Order, and Shine, stay the way they should be—the standard. Visual controls are a major way to achieve the 5S standards.

Sustain

Sustain means to nurture and maintain something so that it will last. Managers and Team Leaders should positively reinforce, or nurture, the team's efforts to keep the workplace neat and clean. Newsletters, 5S maps, pocket guides, checklists, and training are a few ways to nurture the ongoing 5S for Safety effort.

Two Phases: Basic and Focused 5S

In Basic 5S the implementation team will implement the 5S's in order to organize and standardize physical conditions in the target area. This should take about two months. Nearly 50% of the area's safety problems can be corrected with Basic 5S, even without a specific focus on safety.

In Focused 5S the team will identify shopfloor conditions that can cause accidents, correct the conditions, and then control and prevent them. While Basic 5S takes a "fix it" approach, Focused 5S takes a "control and prevent" approach. So it requires a systematic, step-by-step approach. These steps are *See, Think, Plan*, and *Do*.

See

See means to perform a detailed safety audit. By collecting data using such techniques as area maps, arrow diagrams, checklists, yellow tags, and storyboards the team will get a true safety picture of the target area.

Think

Think means to analyze the data. In Think the team categorizes problems into their related "S"—for instance, oil leakage is a Shine problem. The team then chooses a problem or family of problems and performs a cause analysis to uncover the real reasons for the problem's existence.

Plan

Plan means to brainstorm potential best practices for controlling the problem and then select and prepare the solution for implementation.

Do

Do means to test, modify, and adopt successful best practices. It also means that the best practice becomes a standard that should be adhered to by everyone.

By applying this improvement process of See, Think, Plan, Do continuously—first with all problems identified in the safety audit and then through daily inspections—the team will gain control of its workplace.

Measuring Success

The Safety Management Team's and specific project teams' long-term successes are typically measured by a number of reactive indicators—accident rates, incident rates, lost work-day rates, corresponding costs, etc.

Proactive indicators include workplace assessments that are conducted as a regular task of the operational group. The Workplace Scan Diagnostic Checklist and the 5S for Safety Audit are based upon a non-intrusive assessment process. This type of process provides better, more reliable results. Gone is the reliance on assessments that are announced and prepared for in advance, whose results are misleading, and who carry the punitive side effects that are common with being audited by OSHA, clients, ISO auditors, or other outside groups.

Warning Signs

There are common signs that predict whether or not a project will be difficult or even successful.

Watch out for these symptoms. The Safety Manager and Project Leader are responsible for correcting these as soon as they appear.

Warning Signs

- Little or no management support
- Little or no management support
- Little or no management support
- Condition or target that is not significant or detrimental enough to justify change
- Low employee involvement
- Unclear or unfocused goals
- Unclear performance expectations
- Unclear process for project team
- Incomplete data collection
- Poor training

Summary

The 5S for Safety approach provides a step-by-step procedure, a reliable method, and a clear focus on environmental conditions. These tools are meant to guide you. You should adopt them to your own 5S for Safety program.

Introduction

The way you plan and prepare will make the difference between achieving your goals or not achieving your goals. An adequately prepared project is one in which the goals and strategies are thoroughly thought out and clearly articulated. It usually meets its goals, stays within the estimated timeframe and budget, and is well-received by management.

Objectives for Step 2

The Safety Manager, Team Leader and/or Project Team will:

• Prioritize safety initiatives and establish support.

• Choose a target improvement area.

• Choose a project team leader.

• Host appropriate informational meetings.

• Write a project team charter.

Information About Plan and Prepare

Frequent and regular communication is essential to the success of this or any project or sustaining activity. Seek out opportunities to tell your coworkers about 5S and how 5S will improve safety. Opportunities to share information includes area meetings, process improvement teams, update meeting, and even lunch breaks.

Making Decisions

When organizations implement projects, one of the biggest sources of confusion is who has the responsibility and authority for which decisions. One thing is for certain: There is no one right way to make decisions. The following should be taken into account.

- *Information.* Do the people with the authority have the proper information at the right time?

- *Time.* The more people involved in a decision, the longer it usually takes.

- *Authority.* A manager or leader cannot give away more authority or freedom than he has. Get agreement from the level above before assuming control.

- *Responsibility and accountability.* Taking on authority brings with it added accountability. Everyone should understand what is required of them.

- *Boundaries.* Boundaries need to be clear. In addition, a successful organization is one in which decision-making boundaries continue to expand.

- *Diversity.* We all have different knowledge, skills, and experience. Always try to build as much diversity as possible into a structure without jeopardizing success.

Choose a Target Area

Selecting a suitable target area is important for 5S for Safety implementation.

The first two or three target areas in a plan should be seen as pilot areas. Therefore, you should choose areas with a high likelihood of success.

Choose a Team Leader

In most cases a team leader will be chosen by the time teams are formed.

The project team leader has the following objectives:

- Assist in preliminary audit and writing of the team charter.

- Form an implementation team.

- Apply a participative approach to 5S implementation.

- Empower the team by providing direction, support, and opportunities to perform.

- Prepare agendas and lead team meetings effectively.

- Report to management on a regular basis.

- Obtain resources needed by the team.

- Ensure that the 5S for Safety approach is applied systematically.

Conduct a Preliminary Audit

The purpose of the Preliminary Audit is to document the conditions of your work area so that you may determine whether you are ready for Rapid Basic 5S or need to apply an In-depth Basic 5S.

The Preliminary Audit uses the Workplace Scan Diagnostic Checklist. This Checklist is used in all 5S activities. As such, the Checklist is used for both the Preliminary Audit in Step 2 and the Workplace Scan in Step 4: Basic 5S.

To conduct the Preliminary Audit:

- Request permission from management prior to beginning.

- Obtain a copy of the Workplace Scan Diagnostic Checklist and review how to use it.

- Pre-read the checklist to become familiar with the questions.

- Identify the area in which the audit will be conducted.

- Fill in the "Date" and "Target Area" lines at the top of the Checklist.

- Now you are ready to conduct the audit! While walking through the area, record the number of infractions for each line item (Remember, this is a preliminary audit only. There is no reason to be too concerned with absolute accuracy in your counts. The trends in the data will provide the needed information to move forward.)

- Score the checklist according to the chart below to decide whether Rapid or In-depth Implementation of Basic 5S is most appropriate for you.

If your preliminary audit score is:	then follow:
0-60	Rapid implementation of Basic 5S followed by Focused 5S
61-100	In-depth Implementation of Basic 5S before applying Focused 5S

Develop a Team Charter

Step 2: Plan and Prepare culminates in the writing of a Team Charter. The charter provides clarity and direction for the team and should answer the organizational questions a team will have. It also provides a tool for negotiation. By reading and accepting the charter, or proposing changes, a team will play an active role in planning and preparing the project. The result is buy-in and ownership.

Description

A Team Charter is a written document that provides a framework for maximizing a team's effectiveness.

Purpose

A Team Charter gives clear directions, information, and identifies the resources necessary so that a team can create a strategy and an action plan linked to company strategy. It typically defines the scope of a team's work and maps out key elements of that work—purpose, outcomes, performance measures, principles, givens, levels of authority, and decision-making processes, roles and responsibilities, and work methods.

Creating a Team Charter

You can create a good charter by answering the following questions and documenting your answers in a document like the one provided in this section. Refer to Appendix B in the Facilitator Guide for more in-depth information about the creation of team charters.

- Who are the team members and other stakeholders?

- What are their roles and responsibilities?

- What is the target area, what is its purpose and what functions take place within it?

- Why has this target area been chosen as the focus of team efforts?

- What outcomes are expected of the team?

- What is the team's vision for improving the work area?

- What authority does the team have to make decisions, how does it make them, and what are the principles and givens underlying the team's efforts?

Summary

The time and effort invested in planning and preparing for 5S for Safety implementation is critical. Establishing management support, avenues for communicating progress, and defining specific goals are each a critical part of Plan and Prepare. Together they lay the groundwork for success.

Application Tasks

1. Thoroughly study this section prior to initiating Step 2 tasks.

2. Make sure the structure for decision making is in place.

3. Choose a target area.

4. Choose a team leader.

5. Host an informational meeting to communicate, answer questions, and renew management support.

6. Determine readiness by conducting a preliminary audit.

7. Develop a team charter

Note: If the project team is already in place they should participate in these activities.

Step 2 Worksheets

• Workplace Diagnostic Scan Checklist

• Team Charter

STEP 2

Workplace Scan Diagnostic Checklist

Date: _____ **Target Areas:** _____

Category	Item	Date Rated ⟶				
Sort (Organization)	**Distinguish between what is needed and not needed**					
	Unneeded equipment, tools, furniture, etc. are present					
	Unneeded items are on walls, bulletin boards, etc.					
	Items are present in aisleways, stairways, corners, etc.					
	Unneeded inventory, supplies, parts, or materials are present					
	Safety hazards (water, oil, chemical, machines) exist					
Set in Order (Orderliness)	**A place for everything and everything in its place**					
	Correct places for items are not obvious					
	Items are not in their correct places					
	Aisleways, workstations, equipment locations are not indicated					
	Items are not put away immediately after use					
	Height and quantity limits are not obvious					
Shine (Cleanliness)	**Cleaning, and looking for ways to keep it clean and organized**					
	Floors, walls, stairs, and surfaces are not free of dirt, oil, and grease					
	Equipment is not kept clean and free of dirt, oil, and grease					
	Cleaning materials are not easily accessible					
	Lines, labels, signs, etc. are not clean and unbroken					
	Other cleaning problems (of any kind) are present					
Standardize (Adherence)	**Maintain and monitor the first three categories**					
	Necessary information is not visible					
	All standards are not known and visible					
	Checklists don't exist for all cleaning and maintenance jobs					
	All quantities and limits are not easily recognizable					
	How many items can't be located in 30 seconds?					
Sustain (Self-discipline)	**Stick to the rules**					
	How many workers have not had 5S training?					
	How many times, last week, was daily 5S not performed?					
	Number of times that personal belongings are not neatly stored					
	Number of times job aids are not available or up to date					
	Number of times, last week, daily 5S inspections were not performed					
	Total					

Filename: 2_WorkplaceScanDiagnostic.pdf

Team Charter

Purpose: To identify the information necessary for team formation and organization.

Directions:

The core implementation team should fill out this form.

This form should be filled out during the preparation step.

Complete all items and solve any other issues so that you are ready to begin 5S activities.

Today's Date:	**Target Area:**
5S Project Sponsor:	**Target Area Supervisor/Manager:**

Team Member Roles:	**Names:**
Team Facilitator:	
Team Leader:	
Recorder/Reporter:	
Other Members:	

Filename: 2_TeamCharter.pdf

Team Charter

Purpose of Target Area:

Functions of Target Area:

Problem Statement: Why was this area chosen? Summarize current problems and conditions.

Vision: Describe how you want the area to be in terms of safety conditions.

Guidelines, restrictions, boundaries for the project:

Other information or notes:

Filename: 2_TeamCharter.pdf

Introduction

Creating a team-based organization needs to be understood as a business strategy. Dealing with increasingly complex equipment, processes, and customer requirements is a necessity. Step 3 begins to integrate teams into daily work.

Objectives for Step 3

Upon completion of Step 3, the Safety Manager will:

- Review the Team Charter and suggest appropriate modifications.
- Form the team into a working unit.
- Create an action plan.

Information About Team Formation

The goals of each implementation team is to:

- Take corrective action within a target area before someone is injured, nearly injured or becomes ill.
- Develop a shared 5S for Safety knowledge and skill base.

Team Charter

The purpose of a team charter is two-fold. The first purpose is to focus the activities and efforts on the target. It is important to begin all process-related teams with a clear understanding of the problem that is being solved.

The second purpose is to formalize approval of the team's purpose, goals, and members' roles and responsibilities. As such, a team charter should always be created and approved prior to inviting participants to join the team or holding the launch meeting.

When a team charter is given to a team they participate in an activity called "catchball." After thoroughly discussing all elements of the charter they respond to those who initiated the charter—making suggestions for changes or additions. Then they throw it back and the catchball continues until everyone agrees on the contents of the charter.

Identifying Team Members

Selecting the right team members impacts whether or not the project goals are met in a timely, effective manner. To select the right team members, you must analyze what you believe the problem is. (This may change slightly as more data is collected. That's okay.)

Teams are most effective if they have 5–9 members. Teams made of less than 5 usually do not have the necessary skills and energy to drive timely implementation. Teams made of 10 or more tend to be unruly, hard to facilitate, and results are difficult to control.

The following team profile provides a guideline to help you identify your team members.

Team Member Profile	
Number	**Function**
2-3	Target area workers
1-2	Diverse process or area experts, for example • Process engineer • Maintenance engineer • Senior level technician • Industrial engineer • Product manager • Area supervisor
1-2	Safety representatives
1	Team Leader (may also serve as area expert)
1	Management representative (may also serve as Safety Manager)
1	Meeting Facilitator (if necessary)

Figure 8. Team Member Profile

The Launch Meeting

The launch meeting should allow the team to:

• Become familiar with each other.

• Understand the purpose, scope, and objectives of the project.

• Understand their roles and responsibilities.

• Understand the roles and responsibilities of other members.

• Know what the commitment is.

• Clarify issues by asking questions.

• Develop common knowledge and understanding.

Create an Action Plan

An **action plan** is a document that defines the project scope, critical path activities, and specific tasks required to complete the project. The action plan may also include information about who is assigned what task, and when the completion is expected. Action plans are most useful when the project team creates them.

Summary

Selecting the right members is considered the most important part of the implementation process. The team initiates the 5S for Safety process in the target area, begins implementation, and teaches others in the area about the 5S system.

The first meeting is unique to all others. Ensure that you have planned for its success.

Launch Meeting Guidelines

- Prepare and distribute relevant information
- Start on time, don't wait for latecomers
- Be part of the team, not superior to it
- Create a *we* spirit
- Focus on the charter, facilitate "catchball"
- Stay with the agenda, use a "parking lot" on the wall to capture issues and ideas that don't pertain to the agenda
- Address individual problems outside the meeting
- Allow for feedback about the meeting
- End on time

Application Tasks

1. Thoroughly study this chapter prior to initiating Step 3 tasks.

2. Create a problem statement describing the target area.

3. Define what skills and knowledge are necessary for the team.

4. Identify team members.

5. Hold the first team meeting.

6. Create an action plan focusing on safety.

7. Keep a current list of activities, tasks and accomplishments.

8. Communicate goals, accomplishments, and achievements to management.

Step 3 Worksheets

• Team Charter (Completed from Step 2)

• 5S for Safety Action Plan

STEP 3

5S for Safety Action Plan

Team Name: _____ **Team Leader:** _____

Purpose: To organize a team effort for implementation of all or part of the 5S for Safety Process

Directions: - Brainstorm and identify all required action items
- Decide the sequence of actions
- For each action decide who is responsible, the completion date, and methods/details of how it will be accomplished
- Use the document to monitor your progress

Action	Who	By When	How

Filename: 3_ActionPlan.pdf

Introduction

When implementing Basic 5S, there are fundamental activities that should occur. The first set of activities is to prepare the team and area personnel for implementation. These are things that should happen early in the life of the project—usually in Steps 2 and 3. However, you may have to revisit some of these tasks again.

The next set of activities is to thoroughly understand the current situation by performing a workplace scan. With this data you can create an action plan for the implementation of Basic 5S.

Finally, the Basic 5S's are to be implemented. If you have already implemented the Basic 5S's and are performing rapid implementation you can quickly reapply Sort, Set in Order, and Shine to ready yourself for Focused 5S for Safety.

Objectives for Step 4

Upon completion of Step 4, the project team will:

- Perform a workplace scan
- Create a Basic 5S plan
- Proactively encourage target area workers to participate
- Implement Basic 5S, including:
  - Sort through and sort out
  - Set things in order and set limits
  - Shine and clean through inspection
  - Standardize and share information
  - Sustain through self-discipline

About Basic 5S

No matter what kind of industry you work in, there are five basic workplace activities that should be done everyday. Each activity is part of the support structure of the 5S system. The system will not withstand the test of time if any one of these pieces is weak or missing. When whole and strong, these activities form the 5S system for workplace organization and standardization.

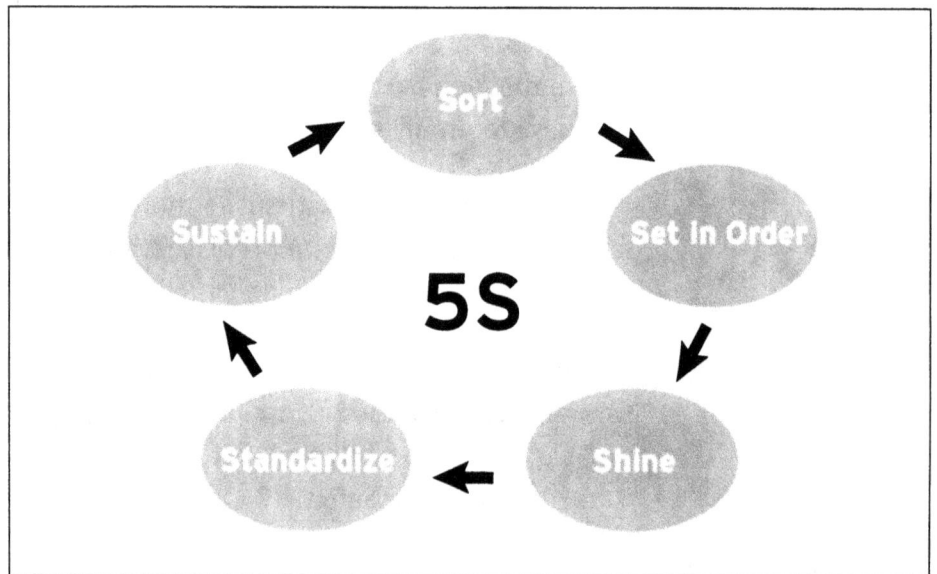

Figure 9. Basic 5S

Sort

Sort means to organize your workplace by sorting through and sorting out every item in the target area. Separate needed items from unneeded items. Move items that are stored in the wrong place to where they belong. Your guiding principle for Sort is, "When in doubt, move it out."

Many workplaces are filled with clutter—unorganized and often forgotten, tools, parts, papers, boxes, and broken items. As these unneeded items accumulate they create safety hazards, work inefficiencies, and quality issues.

Set in Order

After you get rid of unnecessary items, the next step is to **Set in Order**. Set in Order organizes the items in your workplace so anyone can find and use them. Set in Order also keeps your workplace organized by making it obvious when items are not in their correct place. The guiding principle for Set in Order is "A place for everything, and everything in its place."

Orderliness depends upon determining the best locations for items, then clearly labeling those locations so that they are readily apparent to everyone in the area.

Useful Tip

- Setting things in order is not difficult to understand. Think of how lines and arrows in parking lots direct drivers to park in an orderly way.

- Highway markings and information signs are another example of setting in order so that people can drive safely.

Shine

Shine addresses the need to keep the workplace clean, symptom free, and problem free. Shine means to clean and inspect the target area by sweeping floors, wiping off equipment, and making sure everything in the workplace stays clean.

Shine goes beyond cleaning dirt and grime to include inspection. Inspecting the work area and equipment prevents dirt, grime, equipment breakage, and contamination from occurring. Shine allows you to spot problems early and keep work areas and equipment in top operating condition at all times.

Standardize

When we **Standardize** we put tools and systems into place so that Sort, Set in Order, and Shine are continually maintained. The basic purpose of Standardize is to create guidelines for maintaining behaviors and conditions once they are improved.

For example, putting in a little effort to keep the area clean and organized is much easier and less costly than stopping production periodically, cleaning vigorously to bring the work area up to an acceptable standard, and then restarting production. Through Standardize, visual controls and other techniques are used to monitor and maintain workplace conditions before they are out of control.

Sustain

Sustain means to use self-discipline to make the standards you have established a habit. This means managers and supervisors shall positively reinforce workers' efforts to keep the workplace neat and clean. Newsletters, 5S maps of the work area, pocket guides, checklists, and training are ways to promote self-discipline and help *everyone* integrate 5S activities into their daily work.

Prepare for Implementation

Before diving into Sort activities ask yourself the following questions:

- Do you have management support?
- Is your team clear on their responsibilities?
- Do you have buy-in from target area workers?
- Do you have the resources you need, including time allocation for team members?

If you haven't done so already you should hold a meeting that focuses on beginning the 5S process. This is different than other meetings because it will not deal with team formation issues. Instead, it is concerned with doing the 5S system. Adequate planning will help ensure the meeting runs smoothly.

This should be a short meeting that reviews the actions and responsibilities involved in performing a workplace scan.

Perform a Workplace Scan

The Workplace Scan is the foundation of all 5S activities. The purpose of the Workplace Scan is to provide you with a clear and accurate understanding of current work conditions.

Workplace Scan Tools		
Purpose(s)	Scanning Tool	How You Use It
Data Collection	Area Map	Display current position of all items, groups of items, and work stations.
Data Collection or Analysis	Arrow Diagram	Draw arrows in different colors to represent the flow of materials, people, mobile equipment, etc. Use this with the Area Map.
Data Collection	"Before" and "After" Photography	Take "before" and "after" pictures or videos of key areas. Display pictures or printouts of video still life shots on a map or storyboard.
Data Collection and Assessment	Workplace Scan Diagnostic Checklist	Use the Checklist to assess workplace housekeeping. Later you will use this Checklist again to determine progress.
Share Information	Workplace Scan Display	Display information gathered during scan in target area. Use for discussion and continued update.

Figure 10. Workplace Scan Tools

Establish clear boundaries

Prior to beginning any assessment or data collection, clearly define the boundaries of the target area(s). There may be several functional areas within the 5S target. When this occurs, it is important to clearly identify where one functional area ends and another begins (i.e., walkways, doorways and exits, emergency equipment, etc.).

Visually define area boundaries by placing temporary tape on the floor.

Area Map

The **Area Map** shows the present position of all items, groups of items, and workstations in the target area.

To create the Area Map, start by drawing an outline of the area on a flip chart sheet. Try to use a proportional scale that is as correct as reasonably possible.

Add to your drawing:

- Doors and windows. Make sure your map shows the full range of motion for doors and windows. Remember to include the emergency exit and doors leading to interstitial areas.

- Aisle ways.

- Safety equipment, such as eyewash, rinse, emergency shower, etc.

- Telephones.

- Draw large equipment, working from items on the outside boundaries to items closer to the middle. Remember to mark where emergency switches on the equipment are located.

- Draw smaller equipment and work stations next, marking emergency switches.

- Designate storage shelves and bins.

- Designate work tables for incoming and outgoing work.

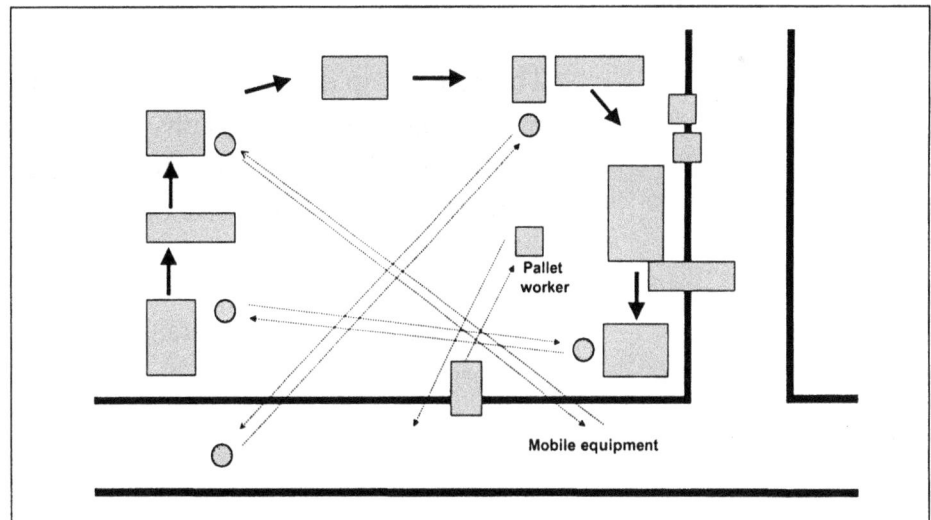

Figure 11. Target Area Map and Arrow Diagram

Arrow Diagram

The **Arrow Diagram** is drawn on the Area Map to show the physical flow of activity within the target area. The arrows should show the flow of people, materials, or other items.

Create an Arrow Diagram by drawing arrows either on self-adhesive note pad sheets or on the map. The arrows should start at an originating activity and point to the next one in the production sequence. If you use self-adhesive note pad sheets, you may easily adjust the arrows (i.e., flow), to test best practices.

Do this for all major activities in the target area. This visual representation will help you determine the best location for the items in the target area and develop the most effective flow of activity.

Photography

The best way to document current conditions is by taking and displaying photographs. Photographs provide a snapshot view of workplace conditions. They are a powerful way to develop a shared understanding, establish support, and communicate achievements.

Documenting conditions before you begin making changes is important. These "before" photographs will provide a visual measurement of the target area.

Maximizing Photography

- Take photos of the whole target area from several strategic locations.
- Photograph major problem areas and activities in the target area.
- Record the picture location, functional area, subject, date, shift, and time for each picture.
- Mount the photographs on a storyboard, area map, or other display.

See Appendix B, **Visual Feedback Photography,** for additional information.

Take "after" photographs after 5S has been implemented. Do this by repeating the photography method described above.

Prominently display the "before" and "after" area photographs side-by-side. Tell everyone in the organization where the photographs are displayed. This is an invaluable communication tool—pictures really do communicate better than words.

Workplace Scan Diagnostic Checklist

The Workplace Scan Diagnostic Checklist has already been used in Step 2 to determine whether a rapid or in-depth 5S process was needed. It should be used again to obtain a 5S baseline rating of the work area as you walk through. To do this:

• Obtain a copy of the Workplace Scan Diagnostic Checklist (you may want to adapt it for the conditions of your work area).

• Complete the information at the top of the form.

• Pre-read the form to familiarize yourself with the content and format.

• Complete one Workplace Scan for each functional area observed.

• While walking through each functional area, observe the area for:
  – Organization
  – Orderliness
  – Cleanliness
  – Standardization
  – Training and adherence to standards

• Complete the checklist based upon your observations and follow the instructions to determine your score.

Workplace Scan Display

The workplace scan is a report of actual conditions in the target area. To gain the most benefit from the scan, create a scan display so everyone who uses the area will understand the problems and issues you have identified.

Bring together the elements on a large display board, then make a presentation to everyone who uses the area. Be sure to ask area workers what they feel are the most important issues and problems that can be addressed through the 5S System. Mount the display in or near the target area.

Create an Action Plan for Basic 5S Implementation

Creating an Action Plan is a useful way to continue clarifying and refining the project. The Action Plan uses the goals defined by the team charter as the starting point, then adds the activities and responsibilities necessary to reach those goals.

Basic 5S Action Plan			
Plant location: Name:		Today's Date:	
Activity	Major Actions	Person Responsible	Timing
Sort	Establish Holding Area	John	By Fri.
	Design Red Tags	Mary	By Mon.
	Set Red Tag Criteria	Larry	By Mon.

Figure 12. 5S Action Plan

It is important to complete the Action Plan after the Team Charter and Workplace Scan are complete.

To complete the Action Plan:

1. Begin by filling in the target area, team name, and date information.

2. Review the scan information.

3. Ask the team to brainstorm all the detailed activities that will have to take place to apply Sort.

4. Write down the brainstormed list on flip chart pages.

5. Continue writing down the steps until all the ideas are written down.

6. Cross out comments that do not apply to the goal.

7. Enter the activities for Sort on the action plan as well as the person responsible, and the timing.

8. Move useful ideas to a "Bin" list if they offer important concepts or ideas that should not be forgotten or lost. (A bin list is a list of ideas or topics that should be considered or addressed at a later time. They are "binned" for a later time because they do not apply to the subject being discussed at the time they are offered.)

9. Repeat steps 3–8 for Set in Order, Shine, Standardize, and Sustain.

Apply Basic 5S

Applying Sort to the Workplace

By now you have a clear view of the current conditions in your area. It's time to do something about it.

Applying Sort to the workplace means that you will:

• Sort through everything in the target area.

• Separate the items that are unnecessary or in the wrong place.

• Remove those items from the work area.

To accomplish these activities effectively, a procedure called **Red Tagging** is used. Red Tagging is a method use for marking unused, infrequently used, damaged, or misplaced items found in the work area. Red Tagging is performed during the first phase of Sort—when everything in the work area is being "sorted through and sorted out."

The purpose of Red Tagging is to provide an immediate and easily recognized visual indication that an item is out of place. The tag also provides additional information about the item, such as why it is not needed in the area it was found and who placed the Red Tag on it. This information may be helpful in determining the best location for the item.

The Red Tag Technique
There are seven primary activities in the Red Tag Technique:

1. Prepare red tags

2. Prepare red tag holding areas

3. Establish criteria for Red Tagging

4. Attach red tags to unnecessary items

5. Remove red tagged items to a temporary holding area

6. Evaluate red tagged items and decide the outcome

7. Dispose of items

1. Prepare Red Tags

The color red draws attention to problems so they are not forgotten. On the tag you will record information about the tagged item, such as who tagged it, where and when it was tagged, and why it doesn't belong at that location. Tags may contain additional information, such as the value of the item, a file number, or suggestions for how to dispose of the item. Choose a format for your tags that serves the needs of your situation.

2. Prepare Red Tag Holding Areas

Red Tag Holding Areas are temporary areas in the plant where you can deposit tagged items until a decision is made about what to do with them. Each target area should have a holding area, as should the plant as a whole.

An important principle about holding areas is that they are temporary. Items should be removed from local holding areas weekly, and items should be removed from plant holding areas every two weeks.

Operating Red Tag Holding Areas

- The local holding area is for use by the target area workers.
- The central holding area is for use by the entire plant and for items too large for local areas.
- Holding areas should be clearly marked.
- Rules and disposition procedures should be posted in all holding areas.
- Each holding area should have a specific person to manage it.
- Red tags and any other 5S supplies should be available in the holding area.

3. Establish criteria for Red Tagging

Before performing the red tag procedure, the team should identify criteria. Often a factory will already have created criteria for teams to use. Some issues to consider are:

- Does the item have a function in the area? If not, even if it has a function in another area, it should be tagged.
- Who needs the item? Does someone from another shift need it? Areas with multiple shifts need to agree on whether an item is unnecessary.
- How often is an item used? The Item Disposition List at the end of this section gives guidelines for items that are not often used.
- If you remove the item, will it really matter? Often an item seems to have value until you realize that it won't matter if it is gone—you don't really need it.
- Everything is suspect. You should question the need for every item, including large machines, conveyors, and things on walls and hanging from ceilings.

4. Attach red tags to unnecessary items

Using a Red Tag Inspection Sheet, walk through the target area and identify unnecessary items. Look at floors, aisles, stairs, pillars, and corners; behind and beneath equipment; on shelves; in closets and cabinets.

Fill out a red tag for each of these items and attach the tag directly to the item so that it is visible from a distance. If you are not certain about an item, red tag it! A final decision can be made later. Red Tagging should be performed every day.

5. Remove red tagged items to a temporary holding area

This frees the target area of clutter and temporarily stores the tagged items until their final disposition can be determined. Machines or large equipment may have to stay in place until you can permanently remove them. Also, remember that the decision to remove excess inventory may need to involve people other than those on your team.

6. Evaluate red tagged items and decide the outcome

Remember that the holding area is for temporary storage only. Use the Item Disposition List to help decide where to relocate items, whether to recycle, or otherwise dispose of them.

7. Dispose of items

Finally, move items to the appropriate locations. Use the Unneeded Items Log to keep a record of what you do with the items.

Applying Set in Order to the Workplace

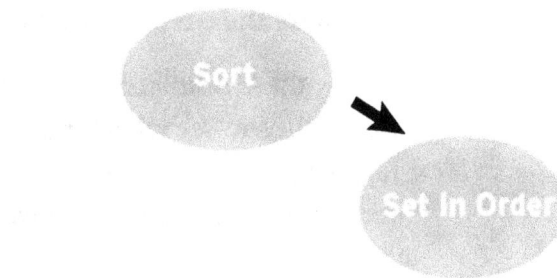

To apply Set in Order to the workplace, you will:

· Decide and organize where to keep necessary items.

· Decide how to keep them.

· Make it easy for anyone to find and use them.

· Make it obvious when they are not in their correct place.

People get used to disorderliness in the workplace, even though it causes problems.

· When aisles or storage areas are not defined, carts and forklifts can run into items, equipment, and people.

· Poorly managed equipment with exposed wires and hoses can be dangerous.

· Chemicals and scrap can be stored in a disorderly or dangerous way.

· Searching for tools, parts, or information adds unnecessary time to processes or changeovers.

How to Set in Order

There are four primary actions for the application of Set in Order.

1. Analyze the current situation

2. Target issues to improve

3. Decide where and how to keep things—and put them there

4. Make it obvious where things belong

1. Analyze the current situation

Review the Workplace Scan Diagnostic Checklist, the area map and the area photos to see whether anything has changed during the Red Tagging procedure. Update the area map, if needed. Most importantly, ask people who use the area where possibilities for improvement exist.

2. Target issues to improve

Begin to set in order the work area by looking for areas where there is a lack of flow—for example, where work flow is delayed; where people, materials, and machines get in each other's way; or where movement is not smooth.

- Focus first on large items such as machines, large equipment, and work benches. Organize and arrange the large items so that there is a smooth flow of production, limited interference from unneeded activities, no bottlenecks, and minimum movement between stations.

- Next, look at storage spaces such as shelves, racks, and inventory pallets.

- Consider inventory, parts, and supplies being stored.

- Address smaller equipment such as carts, chairs, and cans.

- Finally, consider small tools and supplies, including items kept in cabinets and drawers.

3. Decide where things belong

Next, decide where things belong and how they should be placed. Follow these guidelines for determining where to place things:

- The more often an item is used, the closer it should be to where it is used.

- Every item should have a designated name and location.

- Make everything easy to find and to put away properly.

Get things off the floor whenever possible.

4. Use location indicators to make it obvious where things belong

In Set in Order there are three visual techniques known as location indicators that make it clear where items belong and when they should be put away.

Lines:

- *Divider lines* define aisles and operation areas.

- *Marker lines* show the position of equipment and other items.

- *Range lines* indicate range of motion or operation of doors or equipment.

- *Limit lines* show height, minimum or maximum inventory, and similar limits related to items stored in the workplace.

- *Tiger marks* draw attention to safety hazards.

- *Outlines or shadows* show shape and location of tools and equipment stored in the workplace.

- *Arrows* show direction.

Labels:

- Labels indicate each item's storage location and return address.

- Color coding is often effective.

Signboards:

- Indicate name of areas, processes, functions, or equipment.

- Show location, type, and quantity of inventory.

- Show equipment related information.

- Give directions.

Applying Shine in the Work Area

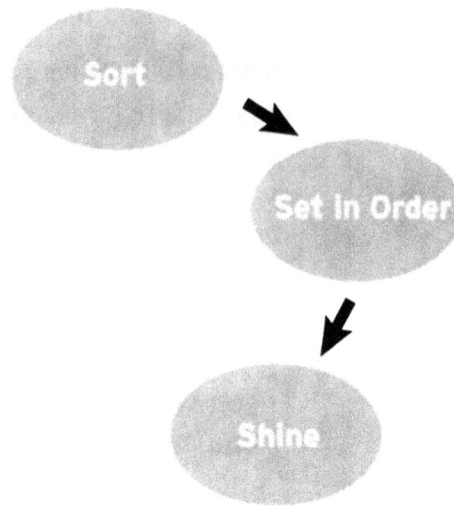

The full meaning of Shine is to:

• Clean everything, inside and out.

• Inspect through cleaning.

• Prevent dirt, grime, and contamination from occurring.

Cleaning may seem simple and obvious, and you probably already have a cleaning routine for your workplace. In Shine however, cleaning is not just to make things look good, it is a way to spot problems early and keep work areas and equipment in top operating condition.

Applying Shine

There are four primary actions in Shine:

1. Determine targets and assignments

2. Determine cleaning methods

3. Perform initial cleaning

4. Replace worn parts

1. Determine targets and assignments

Use a Shine Inspection Sheet to help you decide everything that needs cleaning. Be sure to include inventory and supplies in storage. Examine equipment carefully, inside and out. Also look at space such as floors, aisles, walls, shelves, and other surfaces.

2. Determine cleaning methods

It is important to plan for cleaning so that you have the necessary supplies and tools. One way to ensure that you have the necessary supplies is to develop a "Shine Cart." Use the Initial Cleaning Plan worksheet to organize your efforts.

The Initial Cleaning Plan is a tool that will help you take a systematic approach to cleaning each target area to make sure everything is cleaned carefully and nothing is overlooked.

3. Perform initial cleaning of targets

- Clean everything, but refer to your Shine Inspection Sheet. The Shine Inspection Sheet will ensure that certain items or areas get special treatment.
- Start at the top and work down, beginning with ceilings, light fixtures, and pipes.
- Clean other major items such as machine covers, tables, walls, and doors.
- Clean dirt, chips, oil, dust, rust, sand, and other debris from every surface, and restore surfaces to their original states.
- Next, clean areas such as drawers, cabinets, and inside of machines.
- Finally, clean the floors and aisle ways.

4. Replace worn parts

By replacing worn wires, hoses, pipes, and other parts you will often handle most equipment issues before they become problems. If it is not your job to replace these things, tag them and call the right person!

Standardizing Workplace Conditions

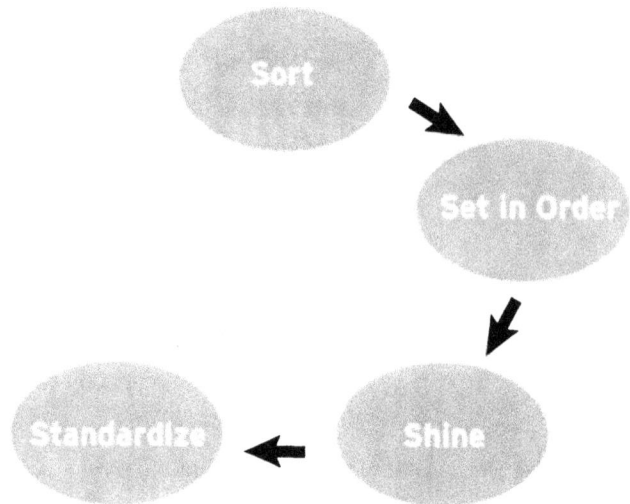

Through Standardize, organizations monitor and maintain the conditions that are in place when Sort, Set in Order, and Shine are fully applied.

Think of standardization as the state that exists when Sort, Set in Order, and Shine are fully maintained. It is easier and less expensive to maintain well established conditions than to stop production periodically to bring the area up to an acceptable standard. The purpose of 5S standardization is to keep conditions at a pre-determined level.

Applying Standardize

There are four primary actions to Standardize:

1. Identify standard conditions for Sort, Set in Order, and Shine
2. Attain standard conditions
3. Make the standard conditions visual
4. Maintain and monitor 5S conditions

1. Identify standard conditions for Sort, Set in Order, and Shine

When applying Sort, Set in Order, and Shine you begin developing conditions for a high performance workplace. Now, during Standardize, you will determine the level of conditions you want to maintain. These new conditions become the standards by which all activities will be maintained. The implementation team should create these standards with input from target area employees and managers.

Typical 5S Standards

Typical Sort standards:
- Amount of inventory
- Tools that belong in the area
- How often to remove scrap
- When and how to perform Red Tagging

Typical Set in Order standards:
- Location of aisle ways, equipment, tools
- Proper location and positioning of inventory
- When and how to replace drills, saws, etc.
- Proper storage of dangerous or fragile items

Typical Shine standards:
- When and how to perform cleaning and maintenance tasks
- Where cleaning tools and supplies are located
- How to replenish cleaning supplies
- When protective clothing is required

2. Attain the standard conditions

There are two main differences between this step and the activities of Sort, Set in Order, and Shine. The first difference is that you are now working to clearly define conditions that you must reach. The second is that there is an expectation of adherence.

3. Make the standard conditions visual

Because people control and manage the work area, it is essential that everyone is able to tell the difference between what is correct and what is incorrect. Visual communication and control techniques such as lines, labels and signboards make it possible to grasp the standard at a glance and immediately correct any variance. In this step, you will make permanent the visual techniques you temporarily implemented in Set in Order:

• Make temporary lines permanent by painting.

• Replace temporary lines and signboards with permanent ones.

• Use color-coding to aid visual orderliness.

4. Maintain and monitor 5S conditions

To maintain and monitor the standards three words apply—Responsibility, Accountability, and Flexibility. Make sure that:

• Everyone knows exactly what he or she is responsible for doing.

• Everyone knows how to do each task.

• Time is allowed to complete the assignment.

• Responsibilities are maintained for completing the assignment.

• Regular audits are conducted to monitor progress against goals.

• Communication is regular.

• Standards are reliable methods, but changeable when needed.

Sustain Involves People

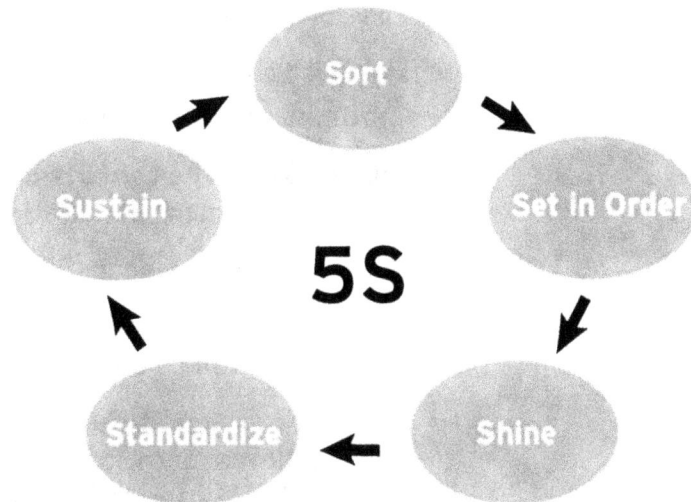

In order to Sustain the changes you have worked hard to achieve, the 5S project activities must become behaviors that are planned for and expected on a daily basis. They must become a habit.

How to Sustain the 5S Gains

There are five actions that should occur for something to become a habit. The employees should:

1. Develop a new awareness and skill level.

2. Receive support from management.

3. Provide ongoing, companywide communication.

4. Make 5S standards a part of daily work.

5. Involve everyone.

1. Develop a new awareness and skill level

Training is an essential part of the 5S System, and there are many opportunities for formal and informal education:

- This Toolkit can be used to train other employees in the target area to participate actively in 5S activities.

- Photographing or videotaping your own examples can help others learn the value of 5S standards.

- Study groups can be used to learn about the 5S System.

- Using the 5S system videotape series is an effective way to train other employees in the target area to participate actively in 5S activities. More information about the 5S system videotapes can be found in Appendix D: Resources, in the Facilitator Guide.

- A full-scale training program led by outside experts will draw in observations, ideas, and study materials used successfully in other organizations.

2. Receive support from management

Managers can give a great deal of support for 5S by providing rewards, recognition, and resources—especially the allocation of time.

3. Provide ongoing, companywide communication

There are many ways to spread the word about 5S, including the following suggestions:

- A 5S communication board is a valuable tool in sharing information about the 5S System.

- Meetings are also useful, but be sure to keep them short and focused.

- A 5S newsletter can be created to spread information about 5S concepts and tools, as well as to share stories about 5S activities and conditions.

4. Make 5S standards a part of daily work

The 5S standards can never really be sustained until they become part of everyone's daily work—when they are considered part of the job, not something extra. Two methods help build 5S into your daily work.

Try the Five-minute 5S approach. At the end of each shift, everyone takes 5 to 10 minutes to Sort, Set in Order, and Shine their own work area. The time can be reduced or increased, as long as it is scheduled for a specific time and everyone participates.

Try the Weekly 5S approach. Once a week, everyone in the area sets aside approximately 30 minutes to perform 5S activities together. This longer session is a good time to implement 5S improvements as well as maintenance of 5S standards previously developed. The implementation team can make these sessions effective by posting specific targets for 5S maintenance and improvement.

5. Involve everyone

Total Employee Involvement provides an opportunity for all employees to become involved. Employees share knowledge and understanding that otherwise would be a wasted resource. Synergies are created that transform a group into a working, self-perpetuating team. When everyone is involved in 5S activities the 5S System takes root in a lasting way.

Summary

Basic 5S conditions are a critically important foundation for any type of improvement. A company cannot succeed at low-inventory production, zero defects processing, quick changeovers, or total productive maintenance in a workplace full of unnecessary or unusable objects, storage areas where no one can find things, and chips, oil, and debris that lie unnoticed on the floor. Many kinds of waste flow directly from disorganization and uncleanness.

Step 4 provided your organization with timely strategies and tools for implementing Basic 5S. Whether you followed Rapid Implementation or In-Depth Implementation, your organization is now prepared to focus on Safety.

Application Tasks

1. Thoroughly study this chapter prior initiating Step 4 tasks.

2. Learn about Basic 5S.

3. Prepare.
   – Communicate, answer questions, and renew management support.
   – Hold a launch meeting with target area workers to communicate process, establish expectations, answer questions, and gain worker support.

4. Perform a Workplace Scan
   – Establish clear boundaries.
   – Create area map and arrow diagram.
     Review the diagnostic checklist.
   – Take "before" photos.
   – Create a workplace scan display.

5. Create a Basic 5S Action Plan.

6. Apply Basic 5S.
   – Sort through and sort out through red tagging.
   – Set things in order and set limits through location indicators.
   – Shine and continue to clean.
   – Establish standards for Sort, Set in Order, and Shine.
   – Sustain through self-discipline.

7. Communicate goals, accomplishments, and achievements to management.

Step 4 Worksheets

Workplace Scan

Workplace Scan Worksheet

Area Map and Arrow Diagram Worksheet

Workplace Scan Diagnostic Checklist

Sort

Sort—Application Checklist

Sort—Item Disposition List

Sort—Unneeded Items Log

Sort—Red Tag Inspection Sheet

Set in Order

Set in Order—Application Checklist

Set in Order—Inspection Sheet

Shine

Shine—Application Checklist

Shine—Inspection Sheet

Shine—Initial Cleaning Plan

Standardize

Standardize—Application Checklist

5S Standard Development Worksheet

Sustain

Sustain—Application Checklist

Sustain—Planning Worksheet

STEP 4

Workplace Scan Worksheet

Target Area:

Purpose: To identify the users and stakeholders of the target area, the primary purpose and functions of the area, and to plan the Workplace Scan.

Directions: Define the boundaries of the target area and tape it off.

Identify the primary purpose of the target area:

Identify the functions of the target area:

Identify the users/stakeholders of the target area:

Plan the Workplace Scan by listing each step, who will perform it, and when it should be completed:

Scan Step	Who	When
• Draw an area map • Draw an arrow diagram • Complete diagnostic checklist • Take photos • Create a Workplace Scan display		

Filename: 4_WorkplaceScanWorksheet.pdf

STEP 4
Area Map and Arrow Diagram Worksheet

Purpose:	To show the actual position of all items, groups of items, and work stations in the target area, and to show the movement of people, material, and products.
Directions:	Use a flip chart sheet, a pencil (you may have to make changes), and Post-its® or other self-stick notes.

Drawing an Area Map

• Begin by drawing an area map, which shows the actual position of all items, groups of items, and work stations in the target area.

• Outline the shape of the target area on the flip chart sheet. Include any doorways or aisleways and use a dotted line to show the range of motion for doors.

• Draw in the larger pieces of equipment, roughly to scale, and label them. You can use Post-its® for this if you want. It is best to draw the pieces of equipment at the outside boundaries first.

• Now draw the smaller pieces of equipment, workstations, and inventory containers. Again, you can use Post-its® if you want.

• Finally, draw in all other items or groups of items, including the ones that are out of place or unneeded.

Drawing an Arrow Diagram

• Next, draw the arrow diagram on the area map.

• Do this by drawing lines and arrows to show the direction of movement of people, material, or any other items, for all major functions in the area.

• You can use a different color for each function (for example, materials delivery might be blue while the flow of the product being assembled might be green).

• Label each function's movement.

• When the area map and arrow diagram are complete, you have a visual representation of the location of items in the target area and the movement of activity between those items.

Filename: 4_AreaMap&ArrowDiagram.pdf

STEP 4

Workplace Scan Diaganostic Checklist

Date: _____ **Target Areas:** _____

Category	Item	Date Rated →				
Sort (Organization)	**Distinguish between what is needed and not needed**					
	Unneeded equipment, tools, furniture, etc. are present					
	Unneeded items are on walls, bulletin boards, etc.					
	Items are present in aisleways, stairways, corners, etc.					
	Unneeded inventory, supplies, parts, or materials are present					
	Safety hazards (water, oil, chemical, machines) exist					
Set in Order (Orderliness)	**A place for everything and everything in its place**					
	Correct places for items are not obvious					
	Items are not in their correct places					
	Aisleways, workstations, equipment locations are not indicated					
	Items are not put away immediately after use					
	Height and quantity limits are not obvious					
Shine (Cleanliness)	**Cleaning, and looking for ways to keep it clean and organized**					
	Floors, walls, stairs, and surfaces are not free of dirt, oil, and grease					
	Equipment is not kept clean and free of dirt, oil, and grease					
	Cleaning materials are not easily accessible					
	Lines, labels, signs, etc. are not clean and unbroken					
	Other cleaning problems (of any kind) are present					
Standardize (Adherence)	**Maintain and monitor the first three categories**					
	Necessary information is not visible					
	All standards are not known and visible					
	Checklists don't exist for all cleaning and maintenance jobs					
	All quantities and limits are not easily recognizable					
	How many items can't be located in 30 seconds?					
Sustain (Self-discipline)	**Stick to the rules**					
	How many workers have not had 5S training?					
	How many times, last week, was daily 5S not performed?					
	Number of times that personal belongings are not neatly stored					
	Number of times job aids are not available or up to date					
	Number of times, last week, daily 5S inspections were not performed					
		Total					

Filename: 4_WorkplaceScanDiagnostic.pdf

STEP 4

Sort—Application Checklist

☐ Review the concept for Sort

☐ Determine the criteria for Red Tagging

☐ Gather any supplies you will need, including red tags

☐ Determine a location for the Red Tag Holding Area and organize it

☐ Determine who will manage the Red Tag Holding Area and how

☐ Create a plan for initial "purging" and get it approved

☐ Purge the area of unnecessary items

☐ Fill out a log sheet of items removed from the area

☐ Continue to manage the first S, Sort, through Red Tagging

Filename: 4_SortApplicationChecklist.pdf

STEP 4

Sort—Item Disposition List

Purpose: To help you decide what to do with red tagged items.

Directions: • For each red tagged item, determine the category within which it belongs.
  • Determine the action required and write it on the red tag and/or the Unneeded Items Log.
  • Take the appropriate action.

Category	Action
Obsolete	• Sell • Hold for depreciation • Give away • Throw away
Defective	• Return to supplier • Throw away
Scrap	• Remove from area to proper location
Trash/garbage	• Throw away • Recycle
Unneeded in this area	• Remove from area to proper location
Used at least once per day	• Carry with you • Keep at place of use
Used about once per week	• Store in area
Used less than once per month	• Store where accessible in plant
Seldom used	• Store in distant place • Sell • Give away • Throw away
Use unknown	• Find out use • Remove from area to proper location

Filename: 4_SortItemDispositionList.pdf

STEP 4

Sort—Unneeded Items Log

Unneeded Item	#	Date	Reason for Tagging	Notes/Disposition

Filename: 4_SortUnneededItemsLog.pdf

STEP 4

Sort—Red Tag Inspection Sheet

Purpose: To ensure that you examine all potential items for red tagging.

Directions:
- Examine all items under each category below for the entire Target Area.
- When you find an item that may not belong where it is, attach a red tag.
- When you have inspected an item under a category, enter a check.

Search these spaces
_____Floors
_____Aisles
_____Operation areas
_____Work stations
_____Corners, behind/under equipment
_____Stairs
_____Small rooms
_____Offices
_____Loading docks
_____Inside cabinets and drawers

Look for unneeded equipment
_____Machines
_____Small tools
_____Dies
_____Jigs
_____Bits
_____Conveyance equipment
_____Plumbing, pipes, etc.
_____Electrical equipment
_____Wire, fixtures, junction boxes

Look for unneeded furniture
_____Cabinets
_____Benches and tables
_____Chairs
_____Carts
_____Other

Search these storage places
_____Shelves
_____Racks
_____Closets
_____Sheds
_____Other storage places

Search the walls, boards, etc.
_____Items hung on walls
_____Bulletin boards
_____Signboards
_____Other

Look for unneeded materials/supplies
_____Raw materials
_____Supplies
_____Parts
_____Work in process
_____Finished products
_____Shipping materials

Look for other unneeded items
_____Work clothes
_____Helmets
_____Work shoes
_____Trash cans
_____Other

Filename: 4_SortRedTagInspection.pdf

STEP 4

Set in Order—Application Checklist

☐ Review the concept of the Second S, Set in Order.

☐ Gather any supplies you will need.

☐ Determine the criteria for Set in Order (for relocating these items), especially who you need to speak to, who should do the relocating, what policies and procedures affect this operation, and when is the best time for item relocation.

☐ Using the area map and arrow diagram, determine the best location for each major item.

☐ Create a plan for moving these items and get it approved.

☐ Move all major items.

☐ Identify and implement Location Indicators for these items in their new locations.

☐ Move all minor, small items to their best locations.

☐ Identify and implement simple Location Indicators for these items in their new locations.

☐ Update the Workplace Scan Display

STEP 4

Set in Order—Inspection Sheet

Purpose: To ensure that you examine all potential items for setting in order.

Directions:
- Examine all items under each category below for the entire target area.
- When you find an item that needs moving, move it to its proper place.
- When you have finished an item under a category, enter a check.

Equipment	Materials/supplies/inventory
_____Machines	_____Raw materials
_____Small tools	_____Supplies
_____Dies	_____Parts
_____Jigs	_____Work in process
_____Bits	_____Finished product
_____Conveyance equipment	_____Shipping materials
_____Cleaning equipment	_____Cleaning supplies
_____Electrical equipment	**Other Items**
_____Fixtures, junction boxes, etc.	_____Charts, graphs, etc.
_____Computer equipment	_____Books, checklists, etc.
Furniture	_____Bulletin boards
_____Cabinets	_____Signboards
_____Benches and tables	_____Pens, pencils, rulers, etc.
_____Chairs	_____Work clothes
_____Carts	_____Helmets
_____Shelves	_____Work shoes
_____Racks	_____Trash cans
	_____Personal items

Filename: 4_SetInspectionSheet.pdf

STEP 4

Shine—Application Checklist

☐ Review the concept for shine

☐ Determine the guidelines for cleaning

☐ Determine targets and assignments

☐ Determine cleaning methods

☐ Confirm management support

☐ Perform initial cleaning of everything

☐ Replace worn wires, hoses, tubing, etc.

☐ Continue to Sort and Set in Order as you clean

STEP 4

Shine—Inspection Sheet

Purpose: To ensure that you examine all potential surfaces and areas for cleaning.

Directions: • Search all items under each category below in the entire target area for cleaning needs.
• When you have finished an item under a category, enter a check.
• You can combine the use of this with the use of the Initial Cleaning Plan on the next page.

Large Surfaces

_____Ceilings

_____Aisles

_____Work stations

_____Corners, behind/under equipment

_____Stairs

_____Loading docks

_____Walls

_____Doors

_____Pillars and posts

_____Floors

_____Other

Surfaces of equipment and furniture

_____Machines

_____Conveyance equipment

_____Plumbing, pipes, sinks

_____Electrical equipment

_____Fixtures, junction boxes

_____Cabinets

_____Benches and tables

_____Chairs

_____Carts

_____Shelves

_____Racks

Inside equipment/furniture

_____Machines

_____Conveyance equipment

_____Closets

_____Drawers

_____Cabinets

_____Sheds

_____Tool boxes

_____Storage bins

Other

_____Materials and supplies

_____Trash cans

_____Bulletin boards

_____Labels and signs

_____Small tools

_____Hoses, cords, tubing, etc.

_____Other

Filename: 4_ShineInspectionSheet.pdf

STEP 4

Shine—Initial Cleaning Plan

Target Area:

Directions:
1. Decide what the task is and where it should happen—list it in the appropriate column below.
2. Decide who will perform the task and when, and list it below.
3. Decide which materials and tools you need and list them below.

Task	Location	Who	When	Materials and Tools Needed

Filename: 4_ShineInitialCleaning.pdf

STEP 4

Standardize—Application Checklist

☐ Determine the condition you want for Sort, Set in Order, and Shine.

☐ Attain those conditions.

☐ Determine the guidelines and standards that will allow you to maintain those conditions.

☐ Implement those guidelines and standards.

☐ Make those guidelines and standards visual.

☐ Maintain and monitor the desired conditions.

☐ Continue to improve conditions.

Filename: 4_StandardizeApplicationChecklist.pdf

STEP 4

5S Standard Development Worksheet

Target Area:

| **Purpose:** | To assist in the development of 5S standards. |

Directions:
- For each of the items below, determine the standard guide-line and/or procedure that everyone should follow.
- Identify other issues that require standards and create those standards as well.

Items to Consider for the Development of Standards

Standards for Sort

- Determine what belongs in an area, and how many.
- Determine what information should be recorded on a red tag.
- Determine how red tagging should occur, who should do it, and when it should be done.
- Determine the guidelines and criteria people should follow in performing red tagging.
- Determine the disposition criteria for red tagged items, including who should make the final decisions, who should carry out the disposition, when it should occur, and how it should be done.
- Determine the guidelines for managing the Red Tag Holding Area, including who should do it, what their responsibilities are, and the record keeping system they should use.

Standards for Set in Order

- Determine where each item belongs.
- Determine standards for location indicators, including the type of indicator, the design of each type, standard colors for various uses, etc.
- Determine the standard procedure for changing the location of an item, including how to make recommendations, who has final authority, etc.

Standards for Shine

- Determine what needs cleaning and maintenance on a regular basis, who performs that cleaning, when it should occur, and the cleaning/maintenance procedure.
- Determine how to make the Shine standards obvious.
- Determine where to store cleaning and maintenance supplies, and how to replace them.

Filename: 4_5SStandardDevelopmentWorksheet.pdf

STEP 4

Sustain—Application Checklist

☐ Create a plan for Sustain.

☐ Ensure that you have management support for the plan, and make necessary modifications.

☐ Ensure that everyone in the area has a basic understanding of the 5S System.

☐ Train everyone in the area about the 5S standards and their purposes.

☐ Create and maintain other communication devices.

☐ Make 5S activities part of daily work through the 5-minute 5S.

☐ Continue to improve standards and visual methods to make all standards obvious.

☐ Continue to improve Total Employee Involvement.

Filename: 4_SustainApplicationChecklist.pdf

STEP 4

Sustain—Planning Worksheet

Target Area:

Purpose: To help you plan methods to sustain the 5S standards and guidelines.

Directions:

- Identify the standards, guidelines, and procedures that require adherence.
- Identify the people or groups of people from whom adherence to the 5S standards, guidelines, and procedures is necessary. List them in the column provided.
- Determine the methods you will use to get adherence to the standards and guidelines and when each method should take place. Consider the following methods as a partial list:
  - 5S concepts and skills training
  - 5S communication board
  - Before and after photos
  - One-point lessons
  - Study groups
  - Information signboards about standards and procedures
  - Daily 5-minute 5S activities
  - Weekly 5S application
- Use the form below to create a plan. It may be best to implement ideas one at a time so each idea has the best chance for success.

Who	Standards, Guidelines, Procedures	Method	When

Filename: 4_SustainPlanningWorksheet.pdf

Introduction

Most of the activities that prepare the organization for implementing a 5S focus on Safety were done in Steps 1–4. You have:

• Completed a Preliminary Audit

• Created an Action Plan

• Formed your team

• Developed a Team Charter

• Implemented or renewed 5S guidelines

Objectives for Step 5

The project team will:

• Perform an in-depth safety audit.

• Analyze findings to determine causes of safety issues.

Information About See and Think

One of the keys to a successful implementation of 5S for Safety is a scientific approach to improvement. That approach is embodied in four activities: See, Think, Plan, Do.

See Perform a safety audit

Think Analyze causes

Plan Identify and prepare best practices

Do Implement

See means to identify all safety problems or potential safety problems where they exist. It's more than identifying accidents or near misses. It is identifying the conditions that may cause accidents.

Think means to thoroughly study the problems and to determine their underlying causes. It also means categorizing those causes into groups that can more easily be dealt with.

Plan means to identify the best practices that will control and prevent the problems.

Do means to test, modify, and adopt the best practices.

Step 5 is about *Seeing* and *Thinking*.

Tools for Seeing and Thinking

The following table provides a brief overview of the tools commonly used to collect and analyze this type of data.

5S for Safety Audit Tools		
Purpose(s)	**Scanning Tool**	**How You Use It**
Data Collection	"Before" and "After" Photography	Take "before" and "after" pictures or videos of key areas. Display pictures or printouts of video still life shots on a map or storyboard.
Data Collection	Area Map	Display current position of all items, groups of items, and work stations.
Data Collection	Yellow Cards	Use the cards to mark safety concerns for immediate or short-term resolution.
Data Collection or Analysis	Arrow Diagram	Draw arrows in different colors to represent the flow of materials, people, mobile equipment, etc. Use this with the Area Map.
Data Collection and Analysis	Worker Interview	Those who work in the area are the best source of information. Have them answer the "5-Why's."
Data Collection and Analysis	Safety Audit Checklist	Use the Checklist to assess the level of safety in the workplace. Later you will use this Checklist again to determine progress.
Data Collection and Analysis	Storyboard	Present all data, photographs, and information on a display to give you a true safety picture.

Figure 13. 5S Audit Tools

Perform an In-Depth Safety Audit

There are five primary actions for a safety audit.

1. Create a baseline measure with a Safety Audit Checklist

2. Create an Area Map and Arrow Diagram

3. Take "before" photographs

4. Conduct interviews of shopfloor personnel

5. Identify hazards by Yellow Tagging

Create a baseline measure with a Safety Audit Checklist

The Safety Audit Checklist is a way to establish a baseline measure of your safety conditions and to continue to measure your improvement.

In Basic 5S you used a checklist to measure general workplace conditions. In this step you will focus on safety, measuring conditions as they relate to safety. You can use the checklist provided here or create your own. Different target areas often have different safety issues. It is useful to create a checklist specific for your area.

Create an Area Map and Arrow Diagram

To help you identify workplace conditions that cause more serious problems, draw an Area Map and Arrow Diagram.

The Area Map shows the present position of all items, groups of items, and workstations in the target area. It documents the current situation and provides a template for testing proposed changes before they are implemented. The Area Map and Arrow Diagram saves the organization valuable time and money.

Take "Before" Photographs

"Before" and "After" photography is an excellent way to document and communicate the current state of the shopfloor.

Take photographs before you begin focusing on Safety. These will give accurate and lasting information from which you may identify immediate hazards, areas to emphasize during the Yellow Tagging procedure, or recurring problems that are so common that they are accepted.

Periodically thoughout the project and on a regular basis afterwards, take "After" photographs. Compare the changes that the focus on safety has affected. Also use "After" photographs to help ensure that the focus on housekeeping and safety is being adhered to.

Conduct interviews of shopfloor personnel

Team members working in the target area everyday are the best sources of information. Worker input not only provides the data you need, but more importantly, it is the first step toward involving others and developing the support that is critical to success.

When talking to shopfloor workers ask open-ended questions. Ask the question differently if you are not getting an appropriate response. Ask questions to clarify and check for understanding. Always assure everyone that this is not an evaluation of them.

Employee Interview Checklist
☐ Ask the area supervisor for approval to talk to the employees.
☐ Decide on a specified day and time. The questioning process should not take more than 10 minutes per person.
☐ Tell employees in advance that you are trying to improve safety through the 5S system and you would like to ask them some questions.
☐ Tell them when you will be back to interview them.
☐ Make sure that you reassure them that the purpose of the questions is to improve safety only, not to evaluate them. Everything they say should be anonymous.
☐ Know what you are going to ask—be prepared.
☐ Show up for the interview at the designated time.
☐ Write down exactly what they say. Do not try to interpret their meaning.
☐ Leave them with your name and the phone number where they may reach you. Often people remember important pieces of information after the interview is over.
☐ Tell them what they can expect to happen. Example: "I will make sure a machine guard is installed on the grinder by Friday;" or "The Safety Team will identify the root cause of the grinder belt flying off."
☐ Tell them when and where progress reports or other information will be available.
☐ Thank them.

Figure 14. Employee Interview Checklist

Identify Hazards by Yellow Tagging

Yellow Tags, sometimes referred to as **Safety Analysis Cards,** are used to mark potential workplace safety hazards. They may be used during the audit or anytime that a safety issue is identified. They may and should be used by everyone.

Yellow Tagging is very similar to Red Tagging. The primary difference is that Yellow Tagging is used specifically to identify and correct issues that impact safety.

Yellow Tagging is the activity of identifying potential safety hazards, marking them with Yellow Tags, and removing or correcting the tagged items.

To perform Yellow Tagging:

• Identify Yellow Tag targets.

• Fill out the requested information on the back of the tag.

• Place the tag on the questionable object.

• Enter Yellow Tag locations on the Area Map.

• Evaluate and correct the yellow-tagged items or processes.

• Document changes and results.

Safety Analysis Card	
Problem Condition:	
Problem Number:	**Location:**
5S Category (check one) ☐ Sort ☐ Set in Order ☐ Shine ☐ Standardize ☐ Sustain	
Control Point (check one) ☐ Chemicals and Hazardous Materials ☐ Machines and Equipment ☐ Transporting Methods and Equipment ☐ Flow (people, equipment, materials) ☐ Work Surfaces ☐ Environmental, Health and Hygiene ☐ Safety, Fire and Emergency Equipment ☐ Personal Equipment and Tools ☐ Inventory, Supplies and Materials ☐ Walk and Travel Surfaces	
Probably Accident/Injury (check one): ☐ (3) High ☐ (2) Medium ☐ (1) Low **Severity of Accident/Injury** (check one): ☐ (3) High ☐ (2) Medium ☐ (1) Low	
Comments:	

Figure 15. Sample Yellow Tag

The Yellow Tagging procedure asks you to identify "Control Points" when filling out the card. **Control Points** are physical categories in which the safety concern falls. Identifying and understanding Control Points helps the team analyze safety data, identify trends, pin point causes, and determine corrective actions much quicker.

Display Data on a Storyboard

Storyboarding is a graphically illustrated representation of a complete story, concept, process, or plan. In this case you will use a storyboard to illustrate all of the information gathered during the safety audit.

There are five primary actions in creating a storyboard:

1. Gather all information to display.

2. Draw a skeleton of the storyboard.

3. Decide where various information will be displayed.

4. Finalize the design.

5. Display the storyboard in or near the target area.

Identify and Analyze Causes

One of the biggest challenges of the data collection and analysis phase is narrowing the large number of items marked with Yellow Tags to a smaller, prioritized list.

There are five primary actions to identifying and analyzing causes:

1. Set up a safety improvement chart.

2. Choose a target.

3. Choose a 5S category for the target.

4. Determine causes.

5. Categorize and study causes.

Set up a 5S for Safety Improvement Chart

A major tool for 5S for Safety is a 5S for Safety Improvement Chart. The improvement chart is a matrix. In the left column are the 5S Categories; Sort, Set in Order, Shine, Standardize, and Sustain.

In the top row are listed the four improvement steps in which to analyze and improve a safety problem. They are:

• Identify a problem or condition.

• List causes.

• Brainstorm best practices.

• Select, test, and adopt best practices.

As you choose problems to solve you will use Post-its to post answers to each of these four improvement steps.

You will find a master copy of the Improvement Chart in Appendix C and on the CD that accompanies this Facilitator Guide. Each team should have a chart that is the size of flip chart paper.

STEP 5

Safety Improvement Chart

Model for a wall chart

5S Category	Identify Problems and Conditions	List Causes	Brainstorm Best Practices	Select, Test, and Adopt Best Practices
Sort				
Set in Order				
Shine				
Standardize				
Sustain				

Filename: 5_SafetyImprovementChart.pdf

Choose Targets by Prioritizing Problems

It's best to work on one problem or a family of related problems one at a time rather than trying to perform a causal analysis for all of the problems that you have identified. To do so you must first prioritize the problems that you have already identified.

The Yellow Tags provide valuable information to help determine which problems should be worked on first, second, third, and so on. A technique called a Pareto Analysis is useful in prioritizing data, establishing and verifying cause and effect, and identifying areas for improvement.

To manage this data using the Pareto technique:

1. Sort the Yellow Tags by Control Point.

2. Find the total number of problems in each category.

3. Calculate the percentages or actual totals for each category.

4. Draw the bars starting with the category with the largest number of defects; next largest, and so on until bars are drawn to represent all Categories with defects.

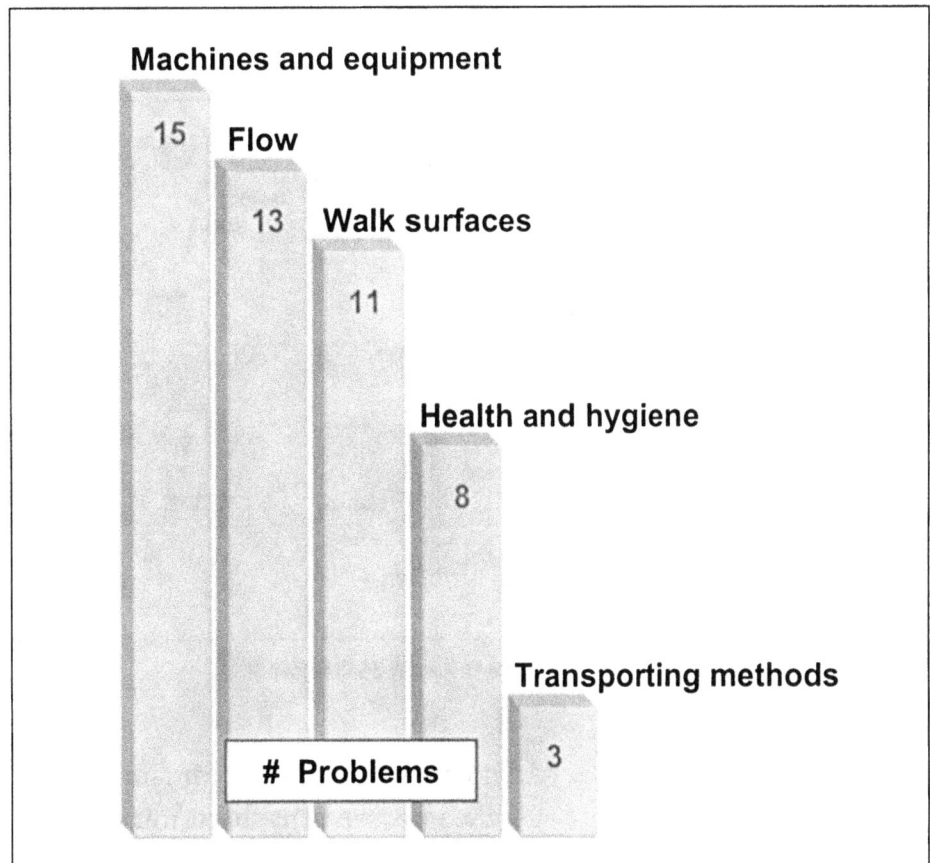

Figure 16. Safety Improvement Chart

Determining which category has the largest percentage of problems is important. However, there are other factors that must be weighed before a final decision is made about where to focus 5S for Safety. Factors which should also be considered include:

- *Resources.* What equipment, supplies, people, etc. will be needed?

- *Time.* How long will it take to correct the problem?

- *Cost.* How much will it cost to implement the change? What is the cost of leaving the problem as it is today?

- *Customer Service.* Are the customers impacted by changing or not changing the problem?

- *Quality.* Will the quality of the processes or the quality of the final product be improved?

Choose a 5S Category for the Target

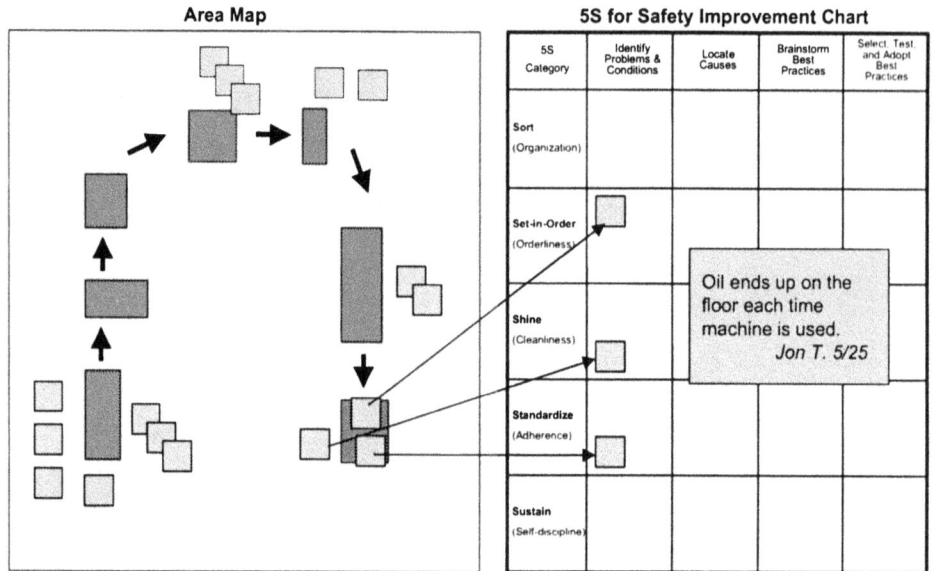

Figure 17. Post by 5S Category

After choosing a problem or family of problems to work on, it's time to use the improvement chart. You should write the problem on a yellow Post-it and place it in the appropriate category on the chart. Use the Problem Category Worksheet to further categorize the data according to 5S standards.

Determine Causes

After you have identified the problems and sorted them into categories, you need to determine the causes of each problem and categorize and post those causes on the Safety Improvement Chart.

You can begin by conducting a quick, informal analysis of the issue. Start by asking questions: Who has the facts? Is there history available? Has anyone done similar research?

The answers to these questions may lead you to the cause of a problem, but more than likely you will need to keep digging. You can use the 5-Why Analysis technique to find the real causes of unsafe conditions.

5-Why Analysis is a tool used for rooting out the cause of a problem. It works to isolate problems by asking questions that target the causes of specific conditions. By looking for reasons why conditions exist, we uncover underlying sources, or causes, of a problem.

To conduct 5-Why Analysis, participants ask, "Why does this particular problem exist?" Continue to ask "Why…" until there is no longer an answer. This series of questioning is usually repeated five times before the cause is identified. Occasionally, you may need to ask, "Why…" more than five times. During other situations, fewer that five may be sufficient to determine the underlying cause.

Categorize and Study Causes

After performing an analysis of the problem you will have discovered a number of causes. There is no such thing as a "root cause." Causes are varied. They have different sources and different levels of severity. In *5S for Safety* you want to discover and eliminate *all* causes.

The next action is to write a yellow card for each cause that you have discovered. Next, choose a 5S category for each cause and post it on the improvement chart. If by doing so you discover additional causes, post them as well.

Figure 18. Categorize Causes

You will now have a profile of the causes of the problem that you chose to solve. By having categorized it on the improvement chart you will also understand the type of problem it is. Solving it will be less complex.

Application Tasks

1. Thoroughly study this chapter prior initiating Step 5 tasks.

2. Hold an information sharing meeting to communicate process, establish expectations, answer questions, and gain worker support.

3. Perform an in-depth safety audit.
   - Create a baseline measure with a Safety Audit Diagnostic Checklist
   - Create an Area Map and Arrow Diagram
   - Take "before" photographs
   - Conduct interviews of shop floor personnel
   - Identify hazards by Yellow Tagging

4. Display data on a Storyboard

  • Gather all information to display
  • Draw a skeleton of the storyboard
  • Decide where various information will be displayed
  • Finalize the design
  • Display the storyboard in or near the target area

5. Identify and analyze causes

  • Set up a safety improvement chart
  • Choose a target
  • Choose a 5S category for the target
  • Determine causes
  • Categorize and study causes

Step 5 Worksheets

Safety Audit Checklist

Area Map and Arrow Diagram Worksheet

Safety Improvement Chart

Problem Category Worksheet

5-Why Analysis Worksheet

<table>
<tr><td>STEP 5</td><td></td></tr>
</table>

Safety Audit Checklist

Date:	**Target Area:**

Directions:	• Record the number of infractions in the entire area for each line item. • Multiply each infraction by 2, then add the entire rating. • Subtract the rating from 100–this is your score. 0 is the lowest rating.

Sort (Organization)	1. Wires, pipes, tubes are exposed or exist where people can bump into to trip over them.	—
	2. Exits, travel surfaces, aisles, doorways, stairs, etc. are obstructed, poorly marked or illuminated.	—
	3. Inappropriate containers and items (scrap bins, disposal receptacles, carboys, carrels) are present.	—
	4. Presence of hazards such as chemicals (alone or in combination), dangerous contact surfaces (hot, cold, sharp, slick), or uncontrolled scraps or waste.	—
	5. Presence of hazardous environmental conditions or poor hygiene such as thermal stressors, airborne pollutants, dust, exhaust fumes, or unhealthy temperatures.	—
Set in Order (Orderliness)	6. Workstations and walkways expose people to moving parts of machines or mobile equipment.	—
	7. Workstations and walkways expose people to steam, hot liquids, chemicals, etc.	—
	8. Storage and stacking of inventory, supplies, and other items are unstable, insecure, and/or uncontrolled.	—
	9. Obtaining or returning tools, materials, supplies, etc. requires reaching, bending, twisting, and lifting of heavy objects.	—
	10. Travel/flow of people, mobile equipment, materials cross or interact.	—
Shine (Cleanliness)	11. Travel surfaces, aisles, stairs, floors, etc. are slippery due to water, soil, oil, grease, etc.	—
	12. Tools, hand equipment, containers, materials, etc. are slippery due to water, soil, oil, grease, etc.	—
	13. Work surfaces are unclean, not neat, or poorly managed.	—
	14. Indicators, dials, labels, instructions, and signs for equipment are unreadable for any reason.	—
	15. Places exist where it is unclear who is responsible to clean or maintain equipment or work spaces.	—
Standardize (Adherence)	16. Tools and equipment have no visible instruction method to show proper use.	—
	17. Number of places exist where it is not obvious where items belong.	—
	18. Evacuation, exit, safety signs or equipment don't exist where needed or are poorly marked.	—
	19. Workstations don't clearly show risk factors, accident procedures, or reporting protocol.	—
	20. Safety, fire, or emergency equipment doesn't exist where needed; it's not clear where it belongs, or it's unclear how to use it.	—
Sustain (Self-discipline)	21. Proper ergonomic equipment, technology, or standards are not in place where needed.	—
	22. Number of employees who work in the area in any way have not had training in handling of hazardous materials or use of equipment.	—
	23. Workers, at the time of this evaluation, have not had 5S for Safety or some equivalent training.	—
	24. Number of work shifts in past week where a safety inspection has not been performed.	—
	25. Personal safety gear or clothing is not available where needed.	—
	26. Number of weeks in a row (or standard time period) where safety metrics have not been taken and displayed in the area.	
	27. Other conditions that are obviously safety problems.	—

Rating System

Total # Infractions ( ) x 2=_____ (your RAW SCORE)

100 minus Raw Score ( ) = _____ (your RATING)

Total # of Infractions ____

Today's Rating ____

Filename: 5_SafetyAuditChecklist.pdf

STEP 5
Area Map and Arrow Diagram Worksheet

Purpose:	To show the actual position of all items, groups of items, and work stations in the target area, and to show the movement of people, material, and products.
Directions:	Use a flip chart sheet, a pencil (you may have to make changes), and Post-its® or other self-stick notes.

Drawing an Area Map

- Begin by drawing an area map, which shows the actual position of all items, groups of items, and work stations in the target area.

- Outline the shape of the target area on the flip chart sheet. Include any doorways or aisleways and use a dotted line to show the range of motion for doors.

- Draw in the larger pieces of equipment, roughly to scale, and label them. You can use Post-its® for this if you want. It is best to draw the pieces of equipment at the outside boundaries first.

- Now draw the smaller pieces of equipment, workstations, and inventory containers. Again, you can use Post-its® if you want.

- Finally, draw in all other items or groups of items, including the ones that are out of place or unneeded.

Drawing an Arrow Diagram

- Next, draw the arrow diagram on the area map.

- Do this by drawing lines and arrows to show the direction of movement of people, material, or any other items, for all major functions in the area.

- You can use a different color for each function (for example, materials delivery might be blue while the flow of the product being assembled might be green).

- Label each function's movement.

- When the area map and arrow diagram are complete, you have a visual representation of the location of items in the target area and the movement of activity between those items.

Filename: 5_AreaMap&ArrowDiagramWorksheet.pdf

STEP 5

Safety Improvement Chart

Model for a wall chart

5S Category	Identify Problems and Conditions	List Causes	Brainstorm Best Practices	Select, Test, and Adopt Best Practices
Sort				
Set in Order				
Shine				
Standardize				
Sustain				

Filename: 5_SafetyImprovementChart.pdf

STEP 5

Problem Category Worksheet

Purpose: To categorize problems, accidents, and near misses in preparation for identification of root causes.

Directions:
- Set up the 5S for Safety Improvement Chart
- Review the yellow problem cards that are posted on the area diagram.
- Determine the category each problem card belongs in–use the definitions provided below.
- Post each yellow problem card on the improvement chart in the appropriate category.

Sort	Problems occur due to items that do not belong in the area, or due to too many of a needed item.
Set in Order	Problems occur because needed items are positioned poorly or put away in the wrong place. This includes physical items as well as walkways and roadways.
Shine	Problems occur due to unclean, dirty or oily equipment or surfaces–any surfaces.
Standardization	Problems occur when no one knows who is responsible for something, when guidelines and rules are lacking, or when a standard is not integrated into the daily work flow and is therefore difficult to follow.
Sustain	Problems occur due to poor communication or training, or when consequences for not following a standard are ineffective.

Filename: 5_ProblemCategoryWorksheet.pdf

STEP 5

5-Why Analysis

Team Name:		Date:

Purpose:	To discover the underlying and/or root causes of a problem

Directions:	1. Complete a problem statement by describing a perceived problem in specific terms.
	2. Ask the first "why." Why does this problem exist?
	3. Continue to ask "why" until root causes are identified.
	4. This process may take more than "five whys!"

Problem statement:

Ask why 1: _____

Response: _____

Ask why 2: _____

Response: _____

Ask why 3: _____

Response: _____

Ask why 4: _____

Response: _____

Ask why 5: _____

Response: _____

Root cause of the problem:

Filename: 5_5WhyAnalysisWorksheet.pdf

Introduction

Plan means to identify the best practices that will control and prevent safety problems.

Do means to test, modify, and adopt the best practices.

Best practices are reliable methods. They have proven to work as solutions for specific safety problems. Step 6 teaches participants how to identify the methods best suited for their specific needs.

There may be assumptions, unknown variables or changes in conditions that occur. These will impact whether or not the solution first selected is ultimately the best solution for you. Selecting and testing solutions to ensure results are important. Step 6 leads the participant through select, test, and adopt strategies that work.

Objectives for Step 6

The project team will

• Research best practices.

• Brainstorm best practices for selected problems.

• Select, test and adopt best practices.

Information About Best Practices Implementation

You have already identified, discussed, and determined many causes of the problems documented. The issue or cause you select for improvement should reflect the best judgment of the team given the analysis and all the information you have to date.

It's best to focus on one problem or family of problems rather than trying to solve all problems at the same time. When you choose your focus it's time to brainstorm potential best practices.

Brainstorm Potential Best Practices

Best practices are effective, reliable methods. They have already shown that they will improve safety in the workplace. Each time you identify the cause of a safety problem, you can choose from a number of best practices that other companies have found effective in dealing with that same cause.

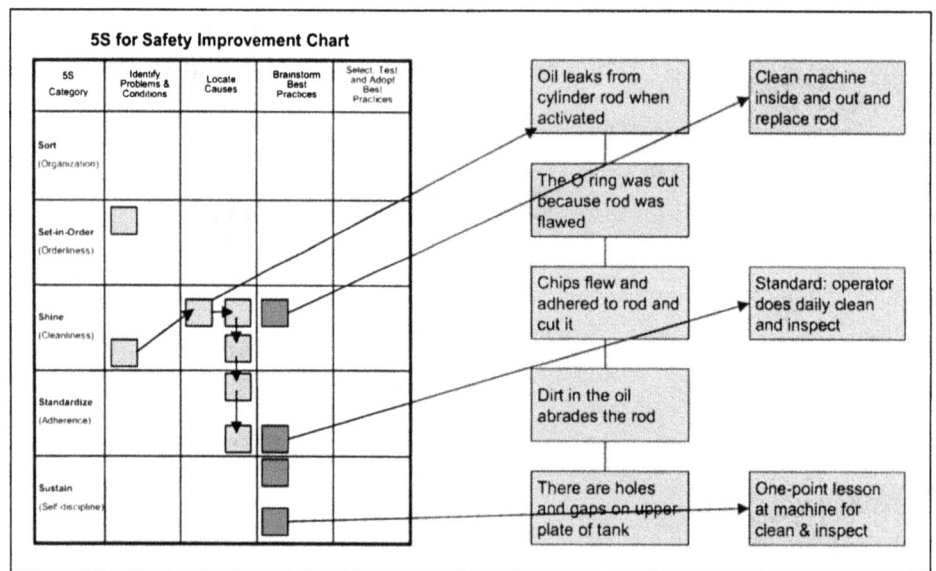

Figure 19. Brainstorm Best Practices

Brainstorming best practices is done by writing potential ideas on **Blue Idea Cards**. Each of the Blue Idea Cards should:

- Express only one idea.
- Use full thoughts and phrases.
- Be concrete and specific.
- Be legible.
- Be signed and dated.

Once all the potential solutions are written on Blue Idea Cards, they should be posted in the Brainstorm Best Practices column on the Improvement Chart.

Another method for identifying best practices is through Brainstorming. Brainstorming is a method where by all team members participate in coming up with potential solutions through an unstructured idea-generating session.

The core implementation team may also use the **Benchmarking** tool. This tool compares current problems in your Target Area with practices used in other best-of-class organizations. Benchmarking allows you to identify potential practices that are proven solutions.

STEP 6

Examples of Best Practices

Sort

- Eliminate the unnecessary
- Create Red Tagging and holding areas
- Maintain a "nothing on the floor" policy
- Eliminate lids, locks, doors
- Prevent vibration, smell, and noise
- Categorize items by importance and safety
- Eliminate oil pans, grime, burrs, and items in the way of people or equipment
- Practice wire management and bundling
- Raise and suspend cables and pipes

Set in Order

- Reorder things based on smooth flow
- Reorder things based on good posture and safe body motion
- Use functional storage based on 5W's and 1H
- Practice putting things away and getting them (have competitive drills)
- Use functional placement for all items
- Use sign boards
- Straight aisles
- Kanban carts
- Molded beds for tools and equipment
- Lower conveyers and shelves
- 30 Second storage and retrieval
- Zoning and placement marks
- Aisle (yellow) and workstation (white) location lines
- I.D. labels, address, and return labels
- First in, first out
- "I can do it" blindfolded replacement
- Preventive covers
- Tools boards with outlines
- Rubber padding and anti-fatigue mats
- Tilted shelves
- Transport on wheels
- Visual indicators

Shine

- Use functional placement for cleaning supplies and equipment
- Make everybody a janitor
- Use visual schedules and checklists
- Clean all surfaces and even places no one sees
- Have cleaning inspections
- Prevent airborne dust
- Use dirt preventing covers and binders

Standardize

- Mark danger zones on meters
- Use thermal labels
- Directional markings and labels
- Voltage labels
- Color-coding
- Warning labels
- Fire-fighting equipment signs
- Responsibility labels
- Smaller weight-limiting containers
- Poka-Yoke devices
- Andon/Alarms
- Limit labels and lines (red)
- Transparent containers and interfaces
- SOP Checklists
- One-point lessons
- Control boards and management boards
- Jidoka
- Process and location maps
- Eliminate the need for tools and equipment
- Maintain a perishable tool program
- Do 5 minute 5S
- Use yellow tiger-striping tape to mark danger

Sustain

- Job training
- Safety training
- Ergonomic awareness
- 5S news
- Safety study tours
- Rewards and recognition
- Tours by top management
- Visually obvious workplace rules
- Results reporting by charts and meetings
- Total employee involvement

Filename: 6_ExamplesBestPractices.pdf

Best Practices and Visual Controls

One of the most effective types of best practices is called **Visual Controls.**

There are a number of ways to communicate. The most commonly used way is speaking. However, did you realize that verbally saying something is the least effective way for the listener to remember what is said? In fact, only 2% of verbal communication is remembered when it is used by itself.

To increase memory and long-term retention, as many of the five senses should be stimulated as possible. This is very difficult to do because our work situations do not usually allow for extensive listening or touching, and almost no tasting. As a result, we rely heavily on combining word recognition with picture recognition to communicate on the shop floor. These are visual communication techniques.

Visual techniques include such things as lines, labels, signboards, color-coding, lights and pictures. Each of these techniques carries a specific meaning. For example, when someone sees a flashing yellow light, the automatic response is to be careful. When a red light is seen, our automatic response is to stop what we are doing. It may also signal that the equipment has stopped what it was doing. Visual codes make it possible to receive direction or information instantly and respond appropriately.

There are several tools and methods available for communicating within the workplace. The most common tools along with their uses are summarized on the Visual Control Tool Categories form.

STEP 6

Visual Control Tool Categories

TYPE	GENERAL PURPOSE
Storyboards	To share information about projects or improvements. To educate and motivate.
Sign boards	To share vital information at point of use.
Maps	To share actual processes, standard operating procedures, directions, etc.
Checklists	To provide an operational tool that facilitates adherence to standards, procedures, criteria, etc.
Indicators	To show correct location, item types, amount, direction, or proper motion by building that information into the workplace.
Andon/Alarms	To provide a strong or unavoidable sign when there is an abnormality or action to be taken.
Mistake-proofing	To prevent abnormalities or problems from occurring, or moving to the next process or step.

Filename: 6_VisualControlToolCategories.pdf

Select and Prepare Best Practices for Implementation

After the team generates enough potential best practice ideas, they should choose the solutions that they think are most likely to succeed.

The blue cards on which selected best practices are written are posted in the "Select, Test, and Adopt Best Practices" column of the Safety Improvement Chart. These items can also be included in a "Success Stories" section of the chart. Doing this will help increase employee awareness of 5S for Safety and document its success.

Figure 20. Select Ideas for Testing

Criteria for Selection

The next primary task is to implement the best practice that you wish to test, test it, and adopt successful practices. Use these criteria for best practices to test:

- Stay within your area of expertise or get help.
- Operate within your circle of influence.
- Get input from the workers in the area.
- Choose appropriate levels of control.
- Find out what works through Benchmarking.
- Eliminate the host—eliminate the hazard.
- Reduce variation—reduce the possibility of an accident.
- Think before you act.

Preparing for Testing

After you and the core implementation team have chosen a potential best practice, you are ready to test it.

Idea Preparation Checklist
☐ Begin with the idea card that you wish to test.
☐ Be clear about whose responsibility it is to prepare the idea.
☐ Be clear about what the idea is.
☐ Consider the impact (who and what it affects).
☐ Identify clear start and end dates for testing.
☐ Be clear about exactly where—machine, location, operation, etc.–to apply the best practice.
☐ Evaluate the resources that will be needed.
☐ Determine how success will be measured.

Figure 21. Idea Preparation Checklist

Implement, Test, and Adopt Best Practices

Now it is time to implement, test, and adopt Best Practices.

Testing

The main purpose of conducting a test for a potential best practice is to ensure that you are controlling the condition that you are testing.

To conduct the test, remember these points:

- Use the equipment, tools, or procedures the way they are designed to be used. (For equipment, this means following the manufacturer's direction.)

- Make sure the environment in which the test is being conducted is as close to a real-time environment as possible.

- If there is any potential for injury, contact your Safety Manager and Management Team for approval and guidance before beginning the test.

- Make sure that anyone conducting the test is fully trained and competent in the area, equipment, or situation being tested.

- Follow your company's policies for testing and evaluating potential changes, all safety policies, communication, and approval requirements, etc.

When conducting a test, if the condition in question is not controlled then either your best practice is incorrectly implemented or you have chosen an incorrect best practice. If this occurs, you should make sure the best practice is correctly implemented. If the situation is still uncontrolled, then select another best practice for testing.

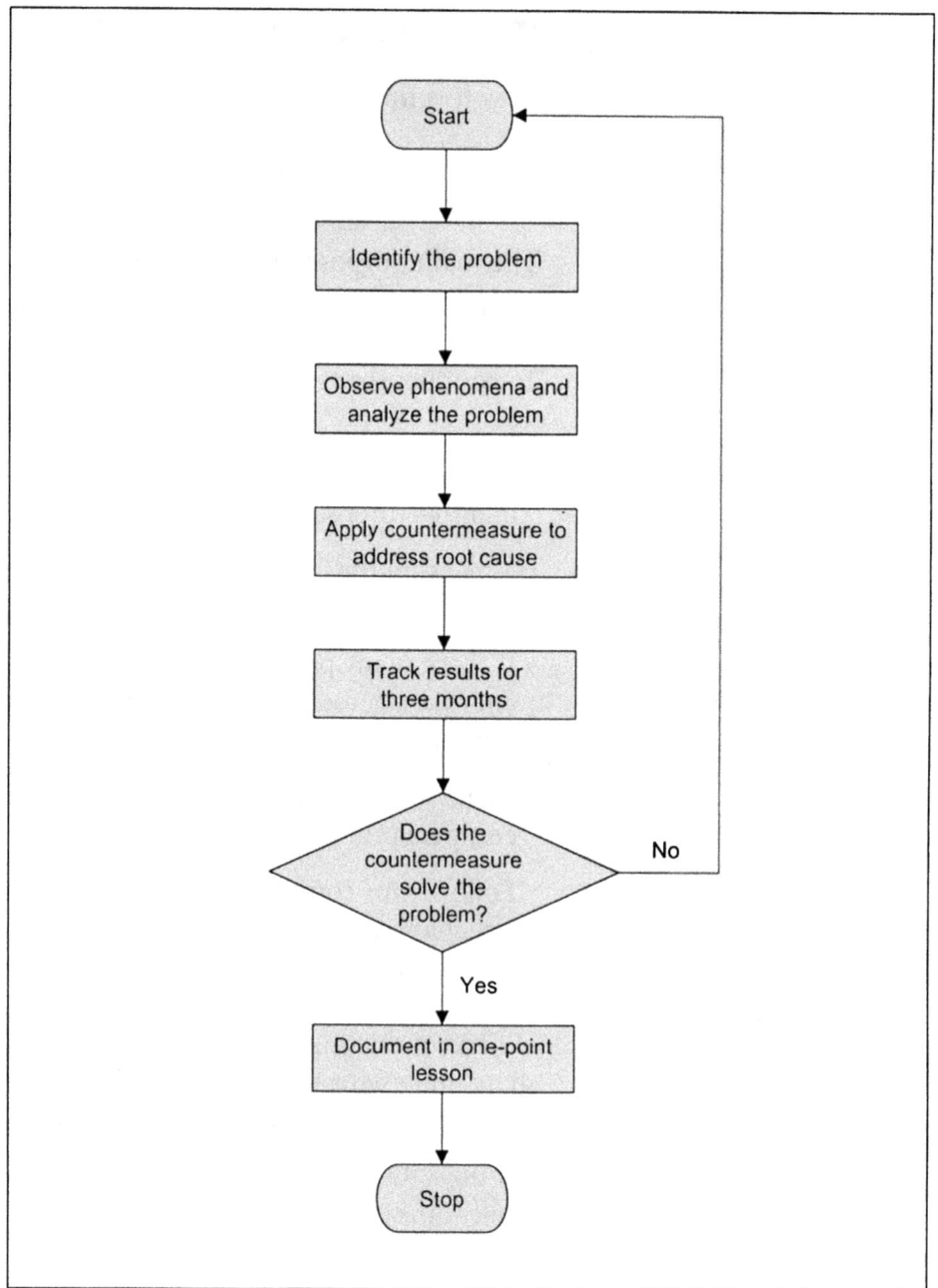

Figure 22. Testing Best Practices

Adopting Successful Ideas

After you have successfully selected and tested potential best practices, you need to integrate them into your normal workplace routine.

The best practices that you adopt can be included in a Success Stories section of the chart. Doing this will help increase employee awareness of 5S for Safety and document its success.

Adopting best practices, however, requires more effort and attention than simply posting cards. Without clear standards, and adherence to those standards, conditions will return to where they used to be. Therefore, getting adherence to best practice standards becomes critical.

Application Tasks

1. Thoroughly study this step prior to initiating Step 6 tasks.

2. Focus on issues and/or causes.

3. Brainstorm possible best practices.

4. Prepare best practices for implementation.

5. Implement, test, and adopt best practices.

Step 6 Worksheets

Best Practice Tool Template

STEP 6

Best Practices Tool Template

	Sort	Set in Order	Shine	Standardize	Sustain
Chemical and hazardous materials					
Machine and other equipment					
Personal equipment and tools					
Inventory and supplies					
Safety, fire, emergency equipment					
Transport methods and equipment					
Work surfaces					
Walk, travel surfaces, stairways					
Environment, air quality, noise, etc.					

Filename: 6_BestPracticesToolTemplate.pdf

Introduction

Maximum, long-term benefits will be achieved if the right system is put into place and if that system is maintained.

As best practices are confirmed to be effective, adopt them as a standard. But adopting a standard, and using it are two different things. Take a moment to consider these questions: How many times have we ignored a stop sign? How may times have we crossed a road in the middle of the street instead of in a clearly marked crosswalk?

Achieving adherence to standards is the final phase toward reducing or eliminating accidents, incidents, near misses, and safety problems.

Objectives for Step 7

Upon completion of Step 7, the participants will:

• Standardize all successful best practices.

• Achieve adherence to those standards.

• Implement processes supporting continuous improvement.

Standardize Best Practices

A **standard** is a decided upon policy. It is our best determination of how something should occur or exist. A good standard is based upon collecting data and information, benchmarking your own organization as well as best-of-class organizations, and identifying and testing best practices. Standards help us control and improve our environment.

Creating Standards—Questions to Ask

When creating standards, ask the following questions:

- Who has the authority to make a formal decision?

- Which manager must approve the decision?

- What exactly is the standard?

- When is the standard formally accepted? That is, when are workers expected to follow the standard?

- Why is the standard accepted? Without a logical, effective reason there won't be buy-in and eventually no adherence.

- Are there other conflicting or competing standards?

- Is the standard easily understood by the user?

The Standard Development Template can assist you in creating standards.

Adherence means that a standard is being followed. The first reason for adherence is that the standard is an effective one. That it works. Not that it works in theory, but that it actually works. If the 5S process was performed correctly, the standard will have been tested and proven to work. Be careful to never assume that another organization's best practice is right for you. Instead, check to see that the standard really works for your situation.

Keys to Achieving Adherence to Standards

- Management support

- Communication and training

- Daily scan

- Regular measurement

- Teamwork

- Continuous improvement

Management Support

Everyone in the organization plays an important part in improving safety. Managers carry a particular burden in demonstrating support through what they say and do. It is not enough to say that they support safety improvements. They must *show* their support by providing for resources, time, personal involvement, and recognition of the work being accomplished.

Perhaps the best way for managers to show their support is through **Management By Walking Around**. Management By Walking Around is just what is says. It is a way for managers to get out of meetings and onto the shop floor. Managers literally walk around the shop floor and office areas every day to see what is going on. By listening to their employees, they can develop a new dimension of understanding and knowledge. Managers can use this time to recognize efforts and accomplishments, and exchange ideas. Most importantly, they create synergy to accomplish even more.

Communication and Training

Another reason a standard is adhered to is because it is easy to understand and it makes sense.

Too often a team that tests and adopts a standard assumes it is as clear to everyone else as it is to them. However, others have not gone through the 5S process and therefore lack some of the background information—researching and discussing the problem, brainstorming, selecting and testing best practices, etc. Therefore, the team must clearly articulate a standard so that the reasons for the standard are as clearly understood as the new, standardized processes are.

Create Necessary Visual Displays to Keep People Practiced

Safety Information
"Do Not Use Oil Here"

Figure 23. Example of a Visual Display

What has passed as "process control" or "safety control" in the past has generally amounted to a post-mortem in which a process or event has been examined—after it has occurred. Visual displays and controls have a different goal—prevention.

Visual displays and controls are an integral part of best practices. In fact, they often are the best practice. The visual displays discussed here have a more specific role—to keep people practiced in safe methods and to always remind them how safe their conditions are.

Visual Displays are implemented to provide just-in-time information on site—when it is needed, where it is needed, and in the form that it is most useful.

One-Point Lessons

One-Point Lessons are short visual presentations on a single point. Generated and used at the point of need a One-Point Lesson is a learning tool for communicating standards, problems, and improvements about work processes and equipment.

Daily Scan

Daily scans are easy and effective ways to make sure the organization is adhering to the 5S for Safety standards. By walking through the area and looking for signs of Scan, Set in Order, and Shine problems you will be able to determine if standards are consistently being adhered to. Consistency is key to making sure opportunities for safety problems are eliminated.

One of the most effective tools in supporting a daily scan is a checklist that is customized to the specific target area in which it will be used.

Regular Measurement

There are a wide variety of metrics that are used in every organization. These metrics use data to communicate whether or not the processes and activities are within defined parameters. Again, consistency of the data is a key factor to consider. Stable data, trends, and excursions (random data points that are typically considered out-of-control) communicate the health of the system.

Data in itself is often difficult to interpret and understand. However, by displaying charts, graphs, pictures, etc. on signboards or storyboards, and using color to emphasize important information, you communicate visually. Pictures attract and hold our attention while easily delivering complicated information.

One of the most effective methods to gather useful measurements is to use the Safety Audit Diagnostic Checklist on a weekly basis.

Teamwork and Ownership

We take pride in our work when it is recognized. Management By Walking Around, daily scans, visual metrics, training and competition between areas are just some of the activities that reinforce how we respond to our environment.

By creating a work environment that is personal we lay the groundwork for ownership, pride and leadership.

By creating an environment that is rewarding and non-threatening, we lay the groundwork for even greater achievements. These are achievements that capitalize on the cumulative knowledge and skills of the team.

Continuous Improvement

Continuous improvement is an integral part of success. All the techniques of Basic 5S and Focused 5S should become part of the daily work flow. In addition, there are a few specific activities that should become part of a continuous improvement structure.

On Accident Training (OAT)

On Accident Training is a problem solving activity that teams follow to analyze the causes of accidents. OAT also provides the structure for teams to discuss how recurrences may be prevented.

There are six rules for conducting OAT:

1. The person who has had an accident or near miss reports it to the team, the team leader, or line manager, and to whomever else such information is appropriate within the organization.

2. An OAT session is convened as soon as possible—ideally on the same day that the accident occurred and certainly no later than the day after. The meeting should last no longer than 30 minutes.

3. The person who had the accident explains how it happened, at the accident's actual location.

4. The group uses the 5S for Safety Improvement Chart to discuss causes and best practices for accident prevention.

5. The line supervisor, area manager, or team leader facilitates the meeting to promote participation by all.

6. Everyone supports an open exchange of ideas and a "no-blame" environment.

Conclusion

The focus on 5S for Safety provides a step-by-step procedure, a reliable method, and a clear focus on environmental conditions. These tools are meant to guide you. You should adopt them to your own 5S for Safety program.

Begin by understanding and applying the basic 5S system completely. It will not only solve many of your safety problems, it will also provide the organization, procedures, and techniques that you will need to apply 5S for Safety.

Don't be held back by our 5S definitions. Create your own, create as many as you need, and name them anything you want. But before you do, understand the basic 5S system.

There are a few keys to successfully focus on 5S for Safety. Following several simple guidelines can make the difference between success and failure.

The first key is, of course, get management support. In fact, managers should do more than lend support, they should set the direction and stay involved. And just as important, get total employee involvement. Shopfloor workers should provide the facts and solutions. Then you will have the full power of the organization behind you.

When you perform your scan and gather data, make sure you do so in the actual place that you want to improve. And as you progress, post your findings and proof of improvement in the area you are working in.

Finally, establish a daily routine so safety becomes everyone's job every day. Remember to keep it simple—a complicated program takes too many resources to maintain and will not provide adequate payback.

Application Tasks

1. Thoroughly study this chapter prior to initiating Step 7 tasks.

2. Standardize best practices.

3. Create necessary visual displays and controls—especially One-Point Lessons.

4. Communicate, share, and educate about standards.

5. Continue to improve, including use of On Accident Training

Step 7 Worksheets

Standard Development Template

One-Point Lesson Worksheet

STEP 7

Standard Development Template

Name:	Date:

What is the best practice called?

_____

_____

_____

_____

Who is responsible for maintaining it?

_____

_____

_____

_____

When and how often is it maintained?

_____

_____

_____

_____

Where is it applied

_____

_____

_____

What is the step-by-step procedure for maintaining it?

_____

_____

_____

_____

Filename: 7_StandardDevelopmentTemplate.pdf

STEP 7

One-Point Lesson Worksheet

One-Point Lesson

Theme:

1. Basic Knowledge
2. Problem Case Study
3. Improvement Case Study
(check one)

Written by:	Reference #
Location:	
Date:	Revision Date

Filename: 7_OnePointLessonWorksheet.pdf

For Product Safety Concerns and Information please contact our EU
representative GPSR@taylorandfrancis.com
Taylor & Francis Verlag GmbH, Kaufingerstraße 24, 80331 München, Germany

www.ingramcontent.com/pod-product-compliance
Lightning Source LLC
Chambersburg PA
CBHW080600220326
41599CB00032B/6549